PERPETUAL

The Secret to Finding God in Your 7 Life Seasons

HOWARD RACHINSKI

Forewords by Michael W. Smith and Mark & Darlene Zschech

Perpetual, The Secret to Finding God in your 7 Life Seasons

Published by:
StarPraise Publishing
7209 SE Topper Drive
Vancouver, WA 98664

ISBN: 978-0-9911311-6-7
ISBN: 978-0-9911311-7-4 (eBook)

Printed in the United States of America.

ENDORSEMENTS

"Howard Rachinski's PERPETUAL is a must-read for any of us searching to understand life's journey and our deeper relationship with God. Howard's story speaks to all of us; through his darkest personal sufferings, greatest triumphs, and personal reflections, he reveals how God gave him meaning through the different seasons of his life. We have all wondered how God can lead us through the lowest valleys and then to the highest mountaintops - sometimes on the same day. This book explains those mysteries; and it is grounded in many biblical examples of how God works in the seasons of each life. I highly recommend this book. It will give you peace and understanding in the storm."

Eddie DeGarmo, Artist, Author,
Gospel Music Hall of Fame Inductee

"You will not want to scan this book. It grabs you by the heart and the healing begins. It has been a great workbook for me personally. This is a must-read for every pastor, every leader, every person!"

Sandra Crouch, Pastor, Artist,
Grammy Award Winner

"If anyone would know the secret of life, it would have to be life's Author. Solving that riddle would certainly be a monumental achievement. Howard Rachinski's book, *Perpetual, The Secret to Finding God in your 7 Life Seasons* comes as close to unraveling that mystery and the marriage of pain and purpose as any book I have ever read. It gives a profound road map, revealing how to process enigmatic pain and seemingly pointless suffering while simultaneously uncovering life's priceless value. A truly transforming read!"

Francis Anfuso, Author and Pastor

"Everyone hurts. Everyone asks, "Why did this happen to me?" Everyone wants to believe, and everyone looks for answers. *Perpetual, The Secret to Finding God in your 7 Life Seasons* is the best book I have ever read that takes on all the "Whys" in life's journey and makes sense of them!"

Geoff Lorenz, Chairman, Lorenz Corporation, Past-President, CMPA

"Every so often a book comes along that leaves an indelible impression on your heart. PERPETUAL is one of those books! From the moment my eyes engaged the opening words until the last closing charge, I found myself fully immersed in Howard's riveting stories, life-changing truths, and personal applications. PERPETUAL compelled me to carefully reflect on my past seasons, prayerfully assess my present season, and strategically prepare for the future seasons of my life. PERPETUAL will make you laugh. You will cry, you'll ponder, and you'll most definitely pray. I highly recommend this book for everyone regardless of where they are on life's journey."

Marc Estes, Lead Pastor — Mannahouse, President — Portland Bible College

"Howard Rachinski has dug into his rich history of ministry, business and family life to help the reader process the seasons of life. But, more than that, they will better understand their purpose in God's plan. I found this book personally encouraging and I do highly recommend it.

Steve McPherson,
CEO — Hillsong Music Publishing

"I love this book! Rachinski has written an unparalleled account of how the Lord uses the seasons of life. It's just masterful. Readers will encounter a very compelling human story. But they will also discover a deep well of wisdom about their own journey — past, present, and future This book is a textbook for life, a book to be underlined, highlighted, and kept on nightstands, work surfaces, and in briefcases as a continuing reference for life's challenges."

Glen Roachelle, Pastor, Author

"*Perpetual, The Secret to Finding God in your 7 Life Seasons* is a great example of Howard Rachinski's love for God and desire to serve people well. His ability to explain the ever-changing seasons with personal insight, scriptural truth, and compassionate guidance makes this book a very resourceful tool. No matter what twists and turns your path is taking or how your past may have tried to define you, Howard throws out a lifeline full of hope that could save your life!"

Jackie Patillo, President & Executive
Director, Gospel Music Association

"This book begins with a limp and ends with a leap! In between, you will find a story of the consistent tension of the Christian experience between calling and character. And, it is told by one of the most faithful travelers and brothers I've ever known. I Corinthians 13:12 reads, "For now we see only a reflection, but then face to face." (CSB) As believers, we strain to see through the veil and somehow make sense of the seasons of our lives as we anticipate the eternal season that is coming. With his story, Howard helps other travelers with the lessons learned along the way. It is the right time for this visionary leader to share with the rest of us. Every reader will be encouraged to keep walking toward the light of eternity and remain faithful in passing the baton of faith to the next generation of runners coming behind."

Mike Harland,
Director — LifeWay Worship

"I highly recommend Howard's book, *PERPETUAL*. A man who has walked with God and persevered through the trials of life to impact the lives of millions of people wrote this book. Howard tells his story and the insights he discovered as he experienced tremendous breakthroughs and victories but also stunning challenges and losses. If you are experiencing despair, discouragement, lack, uncertainty, transition or other adversities, this book will help get you get unstuck and moving forward again. You must read this book!"

Mike Coleman,
Co-Founder and CEO,
Integrity Music 1987-2011

"There is such a difference between telling someone the way to go and a seasoned guide leading us through the valley they've already walked. In this insightful book, Howard candidly welcomes us as friends to his heart's honest journey. As you take the trip with him, your mind will savor wisdom, your heart will be enriched with reflection, and your spirit will be infused with impartation. As a close friend on his journey, I can wholeheartedly recommend *PERPETUAL* to you. It comes from a man whose impeccable integrity and sincerity can be trusted completely. He is the same on the public stage as he is at home. Here he brings a message we all need to embrace, that faith triumphs most when it is tested most. You will always be glad you took this journey with him."

Ken Malmin,
Dean/Portland Bible College

"*PERPETUAL* is a masterfully written book on the trials, joys, and mile markers of life. The book follows the life of Jacob with sound Biblical interpretation and application. The author poignantly and transparently shares from his own journey, the richness of Scripture, and the wisdom and heart of God. It truly is a must-read for all who are on this journey called life!"

Glenda Malmin,
Dean of Women/Portland Bible College

"*PERPETUAL* is a book that helps shape our perspective in different seasons of life. We have been personally shaped and inspired over the years as we have witnessed first-hand, Howard's journey become the message he shares here. We are so thankful to have these words of wisdom written down so that many more people can be inspired and encouraged by them as we have. Thank you, Howard."

Doug and Donna Lasit, Pastors,
The Pearl Church, Denver, CO

"I've known and respected Howard Rachinski for over 30 years. *PERPETUAL* is a real-life documentary revealing essential Biblical perspectives we need to have during the ever-changing seasons of life. Howard opens up his life with honesty, transparency and the painful seasons of his life to give us hope for the painful seasons of our lives. *PERPETUAL* offers life changing perspective. The Father God is being a true father during the seasons of life! I needed to read this book and I think you do too."

Randy Alward,
President, Maranatha Music

DEDICATION

This book is dedicated to
my sister, Myrna, and
my brother, Rod.

Your "big brother" will always carry the pain
of your transition to the other side of eternity.
But, the promise of being together again
fills my heart with the courage to stay the course
through this side.

I miss you!
I love you!

TABLE OF CONTENTS

FOREWORD

MICHAEL W. SMITH

Truth arrives in many forms. Most of us probably think of the words of Scripture as "the Source" of truth. And they are. But, the spoken word, as in a sermon or a song, can also deliver eternal truth right into human hearts. Various art forms—movies, stage performances, sculpture, dance, painting—can serve as conduits of reality.

But, human lives also express truth. The Apostle Paul told the Corinthians that their lives were living letters, known and read by all (2 Corinthians 3:2).

This book, *PERPETUAL,* began its long journey to existence through one human life. Most people know Howard Rachinski as the founder and CEO of Christian Copyright Licensing International (CCLI). But, more than that, he is a man who has passed through various seasons of God's goodness and severity (Romans 11:32).

For as long as I've known Howard, his life has revealed the beautiful truth of our Lord's Life. I've seen Howard in seasons of business, ministry, and friendship. I've never seen or heard a false note. He passed through each season of life with integrity, clarity, discernment, and humility.

Thankfully, for readers, Howard kept good notes of each season. Those notes capture all the glorious, and sometimes gory, details of how our Father deals with those whom He loves. Howard tells it straight. There's not a note of Pablum, "greasy grace," or religious silliness. As always, Jesus is Howard's pattern. Howard tells us that God's "...own Son was also fashioned by the very same administration of suffering as the only path to trust and obedience."

Because of his honesty, in many respects Howard's insights in this book are life-changing.

One of the most helpful viewpoints in the book is the clear knowledge that life's trials are not random or chaotic, but actually fit into an orderly plan of how the Lord matures us. Even in Howard's heartrending descriptions of losing his sister and his brother, he admits, "I sometimes got so caught up in the *now* that I became blind to the promises of, and the journey towards, *tomorrow*."

And with that, this book helps the reader see the greater truth that we don't have to view eternity through the eyes of the temporary; rather, we can view this temporal realm from the eternal one. That makes an enormous difference!

PERPETUAL is not a dry theological treatise; it is a very human story. Trust me: This is the stuff of novels and movies! Through beautiful story and biblical history, the reader begins to see the high drama of walking with the Lord. He, having already been to our future, uses our time on earth as a fitness regimen so that we will be prepared for His ultimate purpose. As Howard tells us, "You may be fine for where you've come from, and you may be fine for where you are, but you are not fine for where you are going."

And, that is really the whole objective of *PERPETUAL*. Howard's beautiful story of God's dealings with two men who lived about 37 centuries apart helps us to see, *really see*, that God will do what He will do to form us into the image of His Son.

He will not leave us floundering around in our failures and weaknesses. As a true Father, He cares enough to prepare us for the splendors of our final destination.

Michael W. Smith
Franklin, Tennessee
July 10, 2019

FOREWORD

MARK & DARLENE ZSCHECH

"The water I give will be an artesian spring within, gushing fountains of endless life."
John 4:14 MSG

Mark and I first met our dear friend, Howard Rachinski, through our kindred passion for worship, almost a quarter-century ago! Since that time in 1995, we've invited him to speak at our church several times.

Why?

Yes, his faith, his empathy, and his commitment to the local church was unwavering. But, it was his love for his family and his commitment to serving God that really endeared him to us all these years. We always knew that God's Spirit produced something of great value in our friend's life. And he would be a good steward of it. As a world class waiter in a fine restaurant, Howard would serve God's people with care and excellence. That service certainly includes the great instrument called CCLI and the invaluable service it has now rendered to churches and songwriters for more than 30 years.

That quality of service is what brought the Gospel Music Association recording artists, songwriters, and executives together in May 2016 to induct Howard into the GMA's Hall of Fame. Many of those gathered in Nashville that night knew what we know, and said what we say, that Howard has always given his best for his Master.

That "giving his best" is what compelled Howard to finally tell his long-awaited story. But, earlier would have been too soon; his story was not finished. It needed the magnificent drama of how the Lord led Howard (and leads us) through His delightful seasons of Preparation, Productivity, Transition, Refreshing, Impartation, as well as the difficult seasons of Despair and Famine.

What Mark and I love about this incredible book is that it shows, once more, there is NO ONE who walks through life unaffected by certain seasons. We each have a choice as to how we will respond to each season we find ourselves in. Howard pours his heart out, holding nothing back as he walks us through his journey of finding purpose through the pain.

How do we deal with disappointment and loss? How do we walk through pain and suffering even when it feels like your prayers hold no power? How do we trust again and yield to these seven unique seasons Howard presents to us?

I believe the Lord will turn this challenging, agonizing, emotional, funny, and revelational book, *PERPETUAL,* into nourishment and renewal for the Body of Christ. The pages ahead contain transformative glimpses of God's loving kindness, goodness, grace, and power. As the reader, you will finish this book much differently than you began it.

You will find so much rich and practical wisdom to apply to your life and to empower you through even the most challenging and stretching times. NO LIfe Season is a waste! You will see clearly how the Lord uses trials and afflictions to open your heart, your vision, your hope, and your trust in Him.

Those hard, dusty, back roads stretching across dry, cracked, and curled landscapes seem uniquely equipped to produce what the gleaming and rapid bullet trains do not. That may be because the walk through dry places takes us near and into the Father's "streams in the desert." He meets us there and gives us water that becomes "an artesian spring within, gushing fountains of endless life. (John 4:14, The Message)

He met me there when I was diagnosed with cancer in 2013. And, through that crucible, He opened that artesian spring and brought new fountains of eternal life to and through me.

And I saw that same Father and His river at work in this wonderful book. As a reader, I was galvanized by how He changed Howard's life and gave him ever clearer and sweeter water. Thankfully, Howard knew that water was for others. And he shares it very generously in this excellent book.

Because of our journey, Mark and I can relate personally and deeply to the chapter on "The Season of Despair." And, like Howard, we learned that the weapon of thankfulness is not being grateful *for* the despair, but rather being grateful *in* it. And, like our friend, we chose to let life be defined by Christ, rather than letting circumstances define life.

And, maybe that's the beauty of God's Presence in our most grueling life experiences. He pulls us further away from our self-reliance, and deeper into proper posture before, and alignment with, the reality of all His great goodness. So, even in the valley of the shadow of death, the great love of God continually catches us by surprise!

Thank you, Howard, for this glowing and glorious testimony of a life lived in the grand paradoxes of submission and gratitude, pain and wonder, weakness and power.

And, to you readers, we know this book will be a great gift to your life as you read it with an open heart. Be ready to catch

His whisper along the way. Just ask our heavenly Father to bring these anointed words to life for you. And then prepare to find that majestic well springing up in your own life.

Mark & Darlene Zschech
Central Coast, Australia
April 17, 2019

INTRODUCTION

The Biblical patriarch Jacob limped. So do I. This book tells both our stories. And it may tell yours.

Jacob and I (and probably you) knew the years of youthful vigor. After all, strength is the glory of the young (Proverbs 20:29). Many of us swaggered when we walked. We did it as we entered factories, schools, office buildings, boardrooms, and down the aisles of airplanes and churches. In our strength, we felt invincible, magisterial, and proud. And we thought those days would never end.

But, then I met strong adversity. And, many times, I didn't know if I was being encountered by God or attacked by the devil. I didn't wrestle all night, as Jacob did. Instead, the struggle lasted several years. But, just as God did to Jacob, He broke my strength and He filled me with His. He did that by taking me through *seasons* of life. For a long time, I thought life had just become impossibly hard. Had I sinned? Had I made God mad?

No.

He was just making me more complete in Him (Colossians 2:10). And He did that by walking me (sometimes dragging me kicking and screaming) through spiritual seasons. Just as God does in the natural, He brought something to maturity through His wise administration of seasons. We all need the winter as much as we need life's springs, summers, and autumns. We don't like the frozen ground, blizzards, broken water pipes, icy roads, and other winter hazards. But, just like Jacob, we need them in order to become more complete, more trusting, more dependent on Him.

Seeing the beautiful order of seasons in life turned my chaos into clarity. I began to see the progression of His ways. Somewhere along the way, I saw the same reality in Jacob's life. And, right there, across the centuries and millennia, I found a "soul-brother" in Jacob. I understood more about him, just as he helped me understand more about my own path.

Every reader lives and navigates through seasons. I hope this book helps you to see your own seasons more clearly.

I also need to tell you that when I look back at the footprints of my life, I am filled with gratitude. I was not born with a proverbial silver spoon in my mouth, but I was born into the quintessential and godly notion of "family." Dad was a hard-working, sports-loving, God-follower who diligently provided for our well-being. Mom was an angel of gentleness who filled our home with gracious love and tender care. Together, they provided a warm, peaceful, and safe Christian environment for my sister, my brother, and me. I didn't always see how blessed I was to grow up in that home. I never had to face any challenges without their unwavering support and encouragement. I never had to fear for my life because of their outrage, disorder, abuse, or addiction (although I dreaded Dad's rightfully deserved, laying-on-of-hands discipline!). I never had to experience pangs of starvation, lack of clothing, or homeless nights. I never had to encounter the pain of racial profiling. And, I never had to suffer the heart-tearing

Seeing the beautiful order of seasons in life turned my chaos into clarity trauma of my parents getting a divorce (Lord willing, my parents will soon celebrate their 70th anniversary).

It was idyllic.

But, even with the advantage of this blessed upbringing within a Christian family, I could not, and did not, escape the heavy and shaping hand of God. Jesus didn't either. The Bible tells us He learned obedience through the things He suffered (Hebrews 5:8). Just imagine that — God's own Son was also fashioned by the very same administration of suffering as the only path to trust and obedience. Just like me, like Jacob, and like you, His "heritage" did not immunize Him from encountering life's problems and life's pain. My "pedigree" didn't shield me from the way of adversity. Yours won't either.

I hope this perspective, as detailed in the pages of this book, will do for you what it did for me: help you see the grand purpose of our great and majestic Creator, the One Who does all things well.

This book is about life's seasons. I have experienced all of them. I understood some of them, while others blew my mental circuits. Some Life Seasons were so wonderful I probably didn't fathom how incredible they were. Other Life Seasons were so stressful and painful that I wondered if I would even make it through them. But, He used all of them—those I labeled "good" and those I considered "bad"—to teach me essential lessons in living. In retrospect, I can now see His footprints engraved on my life path. And, I know where I am going.

I pray that *PERPETUAL* will enlighten your own journey and that you too will delight in your ultimate destination.

CHAPTER 1

A BEAUTIFUL HERITAGE

The LORD is the portion of my inheritance and my cup;
Thou dost support my lot.
The lines have fallen to me in pleasant places;
Indeed, my heritage is beautiful to me. — **Psa. 16:5-6 (NASB)**

In 1985, while serving as music minister in Pastor Dick Iverson's Bible Temple in Portland, Oregon, I read that the Roman Catholic Archdiocese of Chicago had been sued for copying lyrics without the publisher's permission. Oh, the irony: a Christian publisher suing other Christians. And, deepening the incongruity, one song in the lawsuit was "And They'll Know We Are Christians By Our Love." Naturally, that story got our attention; our church was using 400 song lyric overhead projector (OHP) transparencies and we sent out 60,000 worship service tapes annually.

We needed permission to copy songs? I didn't know that. No one knew it. We were stunned to realize that churches could be sued for projecting the songs of our Lord on the wall. Whom should we contact to get permission for all the songs we were using? How much would that cost?

That led to my intense study of copyright law. Of necessity, I learned the whole terrain of that arcane and tedious subject. I came to realize that, for all its great strengths and fairness, copyright law wasn't practical for churches. At a time when churches were moving from songbooks to OHP transparencies, there really was no structure or method to help churches legally license music for congregational singing. But, after my research, I told my pastor I thought we could do something about that. And we did.

At a time when churches were moving from songbooks to OHP transparencies, there really was no structure or method to help churches legally license music for congregational singing.

I began traveling around the country, explaining to publishers how we could solve this emerging crisis. That educational process took a long time, but in 1988 the *Church Music Publishers Association* endorsed our efforts. That gave us legitimacy in the eyes of the publishers, the churches, and the songwriters. I am forever grateful that we were able to serve local churches by providing affordable and legal content, resources, and media.

It took three and one-half years to figure out all the copyright entanglement for churches. We wrote letters to those publishers we knew to be the owners of songs. Sometimes, it took six weeks to get a reply — they were just as frustrated as the churches. When we got a response, the cost of their permission was across the board — some said "free," others said "$60" per song. Our church was large, but just to get copyright permission for the 400 songs we used would have cost us $6000! Churches couldn't afford the cost and publishers couldn't afford to administrate the requests. A real nightmare! The shift from the written culture of hymnals to the digital culture of lyrics projected onto screens had inadvertently and innocently severed the remuneration to composers. Churches had now become publishers and there was no mechanism to rightly honor the songwriter. Very simply, CCLI built a bridge — we found a way to assure the fair and honorable return on their intellectual property. It saved churches many millions of dollars of unnecessary expense and it enabled songwriters, who were blessing churches with their skill, to survive!

After serving as CCLI's CEO for 27 years, I was humbled and overwhelmed to be a 2016 inductee into the Gospel Music Hall of Fame. Even more precious than being recognized and saluted by my peers, I was stunned to see the beauty and kindness of the Lord extended to me at the end of my CCLI career. "Now," as broadcaster Paul Harvey used to say, "you know the rest of the story." Except that is not really the rest of the story.

Peter actually completed the story when he wrote: "Beloved, do not be surprised at the fiery ordeal among you, which comes upon you for your testing, as though some strange thing were happening to you; but to the degree that you share the sufferings of Christ, keep on rejoicing; so that also at the revelation of His glory, you may rejoice with exultation. — 1 Peter 4:12-13 (NASB)

Lest you think that GMA Hall of Fame induction night represents the whole story, let me take you back almost a quarter-century before that beautiful moment. Do you remember the first incursion of reality into your religious construct? Well, here's mine.

TORNADO IN MY HEART

In November 1992, a few months before her 39th birthday, my sister Myrna was diagnosed with an advanced stage of melanoma. She, like our whole family, was blessed with a rich and wonderful heritage of faith in Jesus Christ. So, our family came together to wage a battle for her life; *her* crisis became *our* crisis. We spiritually equipped ourselves and focused our faith on the magnificent mystery of healing. We fasted, we prayed, and we anointed her with oil.

And, in a true biblical pattern, we even saw "signs." The most dramatic one occurred in April 1993. As I flew to Tulsa, Oklahoma, to attend a church conference, I asked the Lord to show me a tornado as a sign my sister would be healed. Why a tornado? I don't know; I was frantic in my "faith" and that's just what popped into my head. Two nights later, while standing on my hotel balcony, I watched a tornado pass by! Naturally, I began shouting with joy. It was 6 p.m. Tulsa time, the exact time that a group of ministers gathered at my sister's home, anointed her with oil, and prayed for her healing.

Of course, with the backdrop of that high drama, I was convinced that Myrna would be healed. But two months later, on June 25, 1993, while changing planes in Minneapolis, I called my voicemail and learned that Myrna had passed away. I was confused and crushed, overwhelmed with unanswerable questions, and completely ravaged by the horrific pain of losing my sister. Like everyone who has experienced such agony, a tornado ripped through my heart. It left a wide swath of total destruction. I asked for a tornado. And I got it.

WHY? WHY? WHY?

That tumultuous experience left a scar on my spirit. People say that time heals the pain. It didn't for me. The ordeal is permanently imprinted on my mind. All of my life's patterns and routines were drastically altered by the loss of Myrna. And, the aftermath became a desperate search for emotional, mental, spiritual, and physical stability.

For the next 10 months, I felt trapped in a vortex of shipwrecked faith, trying to act "normal" on the outside, but lost and empty on the inside. Demonic accusations tormented my mind; "There was a reason that Myrna died. She died because your family didn't have enough faith. She died because of secret sin. She died because of God's punishment." Was I to blame? Was she to blame? Were we all to blame? Fear, guilt, shame, and doubt haunted me. My heart was hollow; I was one "shell-of-a-Christian!" And I was the CEO of a large international Christian company! Naturally, some of those leaders who stood close to me became concerned about the effect of my grief on the business. And, I understood; when King David grieved the death of his son, Absalom, Joab (the captain of the king's army) told David that his behavior was shaming all those who were following him. Basically, Joab told David to "smarten up." They told me the same thing; since people were watching me, I needed to be an "example."

> I felt trapped in a vortex of shipwrecked faith, trying to act "normal" on the outside, but completely lost and empty on the inside.

So, I tried to act like the leader that so many saw me to be. I tried to cover my deep pain and grieve in an "acceptable" fashion. I stayed very busy being a Christian. But, I felt like a hamster feverishly spinning the wheel, running very fast but getting nowhere. My smile was simply a weak and false attempt to hide the toxins in my spirit. I couldn't talk to others about it; I couldn't even utter her name. I couldn't pray, read His Word, or worship. And, I certainly couldn't thank Him.

One year later, in April 1994, I once again flew to Tulsa to attend that same annual conference. And on a Friday afternoon, in the same hotel where I saw my "sign" the year before, I found myself on my knees beside my bed. For the first time in 10 months, I began to thank the Lord. For two hours, a torrent of tears poured down my face as I lifted my hands and began to express my love and gratitude to Him. I emptied everything and unabashedly began to praise the Lord. I felt so light, so relieved, and so expecting that the Lord was going to do something special in the service that evening.

So, with a heart full of newfound hope, I went to the evening service, where the host pastor seated me on the front row. I was ready; I was expectant. What was God going to say? What was He going to do? My spirit seemed to hold its breath with hushed anticipation. Then the host pastor went to the podium and said, "Before we start our service tonight, I would like to introduce my sister, who was diagnosed with melanoma six months ago, and the Lord has healed her."

WHAT???

That pastor's words detonated like a bomb in the deep recesses of my soul, and every spiritual sense within me convulsed into numbness. The concussion of that announcement shredded me. How could God do such a horrible thing to ME? I had finally opened up my heart to Him after 10 months, and that was how He paid me back? He rubbed my sister's death in my face by healing my friend's sister. Of the same disease! I felt humiliated and abandoned; God's "sadistic joke" devastated me. I had summoned the courage to once again expose my "open" heart to God, and in my moment of vulnerability, I felt He had humiliated me!

The next day, as I drove to the Tulsa airport, I growled my contempt to God.

"Go ahead, God; take my life!" I was frustrated, I was confused, and I was angry.

> The next day, as I drove to the Tulsa airport, I growled my contempt to God. "Go ahead, God...take my life!" I was frustrated, I was confused, and I was angry.

A few minutes after my angry outburst at God, a flatbed truck carrying a car body came toward me in the other lane. Then, in slow motion, I watched as the securing straps detached, and the wind lifted the car body off the truck bed and hurled it straight at me. Just before the inevitable impact, my car passed a concrete pillar. At that moment, that concrete pillar took the full blow of the car body. I drove on to the airport. My rental car was untouched. But I was totaled.

I was scared, terrified—God was taking me up on my dare! I called my wife, Donna, and asked her to pray for me.

THE WHISPERS OF HIS LOVE

For the next several hours on that flight, I cried out to God. I sincerely repented; I asked Him to forgive me for my arrogant ignorance. I told Him I was lost and confused. And that is how my desperate search for a true foundation for my faith began. Over the next 12 months, I continuously asked God to clear the clutter of my mental, emotional, and spiritual ugliness. I couldn't put the pieces of my life puzzle together. I had to cast off the rationalism of my own understanding and search for Him. I had to find Him.

I did not find Him immediately or in a single moment or event. But, little by little and piece by piece, I began to hear His whisper in my spirit again. The first real sound of His Presence was in October 1995, a full year and a half after I started reaching out for Him. That's when I met Bishop Frank Retief, Senior Pastor of St. James Church in Cape Town, South Africa. In the middle of my explanation of the ministry that my company, Christian Copyright Licensing International, Inc. (CCLI), provided churches around the world, Bishop Retief interrupted me by saying, "Howard, I believe the Lord wants me to give you this book."

"Howard, it is OK to not feel like praying while you recover from your trauma." – *Bishop Frank Retief*

He handed me *"Tragedy To Triumph—A Christian Response To Trials And Suffering."*[1] Bishop Retief had written the book about a wild shooting spree that had erupted in his church during apartheid. Eleven of his congregants died, and 55 were injured. The horrible event occurred July 25, 1993, exactly 30 days after my sister had passed away. After handing me the book, the bishop made a statement that sent a shock through my spiritual nerves—"Howard, it is OK to not feel like praying while you recover from your trauma." I had shared nothing with him about my journey.

I politely mumbled my thanks for the book and for his spiritual discernment. His words had sliced through the root of blame that had been secretly planted in my heart. No one had ever told me it was OK to feel what I did! Later that night I read the whole book. That's when I started to step out of the quagmire of my confusion. Something happened deep in my spirit when I read this passage from the bishop's book:

> "The loss of confidence after a traumatic event is a well-known phenomenon...Christians do not escape the consequences of trauma. After the massacre in our church, one of the most common complaints by Christians was 'I can't pray.' Maybe you have felt the same way. Your old confidence in going to God in prayer has deserted you...A loss of spiritual orientation is quite normal during and after times of great stress...For Christians, the apparent loss of a sense of God's presence is often the most distressing aspect of suffering..."[2]

Through the bishop's words, I saw that I had allowed myself to become estranged from His Presence; I could not have a "real" conversation with Him. Somehow, I had interpreted my circumstances as evidence or a measurement of God's love and care for me. I had drifted into translating my circumstances as confirmations of the "blessing" for obedience and the "cursing" for disobedience. I had been carrying an unnecessary burden of religious baggage.

After years of Christian rationalism, I was beginning to see a glimmer of light, and hope, and true faith. The process of recovery had begun.

CHAPTER 2

LIFE SEASONS

I am not the "answer man." I face the same hounding questions that everyone faces. Why do I even exist? What's the point of my life? Where am I going? I am simply trying to get through life!

Life often reminds me of the game Zorbing. Zorbing is a recreational sport where players are inside a large air-filled "zorb" (a clear inflated ball about 8 to 10 feet in diameter) and you run as the orb rolls. Going downhill, you can roll so fast that you start bouncing uncontrollably inside the orb. Going uphill, you strain and sweat in order to make any progress. And should you stop trying to make progress, well, reverse flipping uncontrollably is just not a pretty sight! Life, like zorbing, often feels out of our control. And, in life, it is very easy to get completely disoriented — you can lose track of where you've come from, where you are, and where you are going.

We all want our life to count for something. So, we often find ourselves in the perpetual pursuit of trying to be something. Or someone. We spend many hours and dollars beautifying our image and justifying our self-worth. We become possessed with the paranoia of perfection. I guess that's why we all tend to compare our life with others. And that always leads to false conclusions about life.

Why do bad things happen to good people, and good things happen to bad people? Sometimes, you and I can't figure life out.

The musician Asaph expressed the same exasperating frustrations; he even wrote a song about it (Psalm 73:11-14 MSG):

"What's going on here? Is God out to lunch? Nobody's tending the store. The wicked get by with everything; they have it made, piling up riches. I've been stupid to play by the rules; what has it gotten me? A long run of bad luck, that's what-- a slap in the face every time I walk out the door. If I'd have given in and talked like this, I would have betrayed your dear children. Still, when I tried to figure it out, all I got was a splitting headache . . . Until I entered the sanctuary of God. Then I saw the whole picture..."

I had been viewing eternity through the eyes of the temporary, instead of seeing the temporal realm from the eternal one.

Every time we consider the big questions, we should remember the mystery only unlocks when we get into His Presence!

As David wrote in Psalm 16:11(NIV), *"You make known to me the path of life; you will fill me with joy in your presence, with eternal pleasures at your right hand."* Life is a journey, and God will reveal certain milestones along the journey that lead me to Him. No matter what milestone marks my journey, I can embrace joy in and during that moment.

Furthermore, in Philippians 4:11, the Apostle Paul wrote, "...*I have learned to be content whatever the circumstances* (NIV)..." In other words, it doesn't matter which milestone moment I've just passed in my journey; I can find a place of peace and value there.

IS THIS "JUST LIFE" OR JUST A SEASON?

As I reflect back on that period of agony that began almost 30 years ago, I now see that my perspective on life and faith was myopic and incomplete. I had been viewing eternity through the eyes of the temporary, instead of seeing the temporal realm from the eternal one. And, because of that, I was short-circuiting my life's ultimate purpose by aligning it with (and confining it to) my circumstances. I had interpreted one specific segment of my life as being my whole life! But that period of agony was just a "season" of my life.

As my walk into the light continued, I happened to read 1 John 2:12 — 14, which beautifully illustrates the progression of life's journey in Christ. We all begin as newborn babes; we have no strength, experience, or wisdom. We need everything done for us so we can simply survive. We then progress to an age of greater independence, where we can feed and clothe ourselves, and talk and walk with no difficulty.

As we age, life turns into a sequence of events and circumstances that require us to exercise our faith and engage in conflict. And, the results of those conflicts will make us mature, wise, and blessed, or they will relegate us to the chaos of immaturity.

Great! That passage revealed the shallows of my own Christianity; my personal "Life Report Card" embarrassed me! How could I—a follower of Christ since I was six, a graduate of Bible school, a pastor and worship leader, a founder of a global music ministry, and a passionate leader for Him—be considered as "undeveloped" in my Christian faith? It was time for a "come to Jesus" moment.

As I began to look at my life's journey to date, I saw three keys.

First, I realized that my life had comprised a variety of "seasons," when events and circumstances had different emphases. Some of those seasons were pleasant, while others were painful.

I wished some of these seasons could last forever, while others couldn't stop soon enough. I realized that it was easy to misread the whole scope of life while being caught in a single specific season. I sometimes got so caught up in the *now* that I became blind to the promises of, and the journey towards, *tomorrow*.

Second, I began to understand a very important "Life-Value" — How I respond to (and go through) my Life Seasons will determine how I fulfill who He has called me to be. We all go through events and circumstances that profoundly impact our lives. And, whatever we may achieve in life is not because of *what* we went through, but *how* we went through it.

It was easy to misinterpret the whole essence of life while being caught in the parameters of a single specific season.

The death of my sister, and other crucibles, made me feel like I was alone, isolated, and helpless. Those crises made me feel like I was the only one that ever faced such an experience. I was convinced that no one else could possibly understand what I was going through. But, of course, losing a loved one was not exclusive to my life. It has been, is, and will be experienced every day by many people. That loss is painful—we hurt deeply because we love deeply. Those events and circumstances will impact us, cultivate us, and move us into either maturity or immaturity.

Finally, I had been interpreting my circumstances as indicating God's affection or anger. I had been in a performance pattern with God. If I do good, He loves me… and if I do bad, He punishes me. I had misinterpreted the bad events in my life as being a punishment from God because He was mad at me. I couldn't grasp God's love for me until I had children of my own. I discovered a monumental truth: Even if or when my child's behavior breached our relationship of trust, I still deeply loved my child. Their actions did not change my love for them one bit!

Psalm 63:3 (NKJV) says, "Because Your lovingkindness is better than life, my lips shall praise You." The New Living Translation says it this way: "Your unfailing love is better than life itself..." By His Mercy, God has an unfailing love for me! I didn't "earn" His love, and I didn't "deserve" His love. He had loved me before I took my first breath, and He will love me when I take my final breath. I was not a mistake by Him, nor a regret to Him. My physical existence on earth is not my entire life; it is simply a provisional container for who I really am, a living soul, masterfully created by His love. I finally came to a place of embracing this fact—my hard and trying circumstances did not, and do not, and will not imply that God has changed His love for me! And, God's love has a specific plan for me.

I didn't "earn" His love, and I didn't "deserve" His love. He loved me before I took my first breath, and He will love me when I take my final breath. I was not a mistake by Him, nor a regret to Him.

WHAT IS A "SEASON"?

We commonly associate the term "season" with the four divisions of the year— spring, summer, fall, and winter. Each one is determined by the Earth's angle toward the sun. As the tilt changes, the season also changes. Each season displays unique wind, temperature, precipitation patterns, and differing daylight hours. I live in the Northwest U.S. where, in the summer, we have daylight until after 9 p.m. And, it only rains once a year—from October to May!

Each of these seasons will bring a different influence to vegetation growth cycles. One season will find you planting and cultivating, another season will call for harvesting, and another season is for pruning and preparing the ground for a future season. Each season may have different colors, from the white and pink blossoms of a "starting" season to the yellow, orange, and red leaves of a "closing" season. Each season has a unique value, and we can see it if we look for it.

One irrefutable fact about seasons is that they will always come and they will always go! God made this an absolute when He declared in Genesis 8:22 – "As long as the earth remains, there will be planting and harvest, cold and heat, summer and winter, day and night."

In the spring, I feel myself coming alive with the unfolding of newness, the blossoms, the leaves, and the clearing of the skies. In the summer, I love to feel the embracing radiance of the sun as I dutifully battle on the mission fields of the golf course. In the fall, I enjoy sensing the crispness in the air and watching the eruption of color in the trees. In the winter, I do my snow dance in the hush of the majestic white silence.

Solomon, who experienced many seasons in his life, wrote, "*To everything there is a season, a time for every purpose under heaven.*" (Ecclesiastes 3:1NKJV) John Wesley said that a season was "*a certain time appointed by God for its being and continuance, which no human wit or providence can alter.*"[3]

When Paul wrote to the Thessalonians about "times" and "seasons," (1 Thessalonians 5:1), the words he used can help our understanding of Life Seasons. First, "times" is an English translation of the Greek word "Chronos," which is where we get the word "chronology." It lays out events, activities, and dates in their order of occurrence. And, "seasons" in that passage derives from the Greek word "Kairos," which means an occasion, appointment, a set or proper parameter of time.

It is important to understand that a Life Season is not governed by a calendar ("*Chronos*"); it is governed by a divine appointment ("*Kairos*"). Regardless of your age, gender, ethnicity, or social status, you will experience Life Seasons according to His Purpose in, and for, you!

One irrefutable fact about seasons is that they will always come, and they will always go. God made this an absolute certainty when He declared in Genesis 8:22 (NLT) — "As long as the earth remains, there will be planting and harvest, cold and heat, summer and winter, day and night."

So, as with nature, our personal Life Seasons are also marked by unique characteristics and emphases. And they will always begin and end.

WHAT IS THE PURPOSE OF A LIFE SEASON?

A Life Season is a period of time in our journey, marked by certain conditions, circumstances, or activities. Each Life Season carries a focus and purpose that, when woven together with all of our Life Seasons, makes its own unique contribution to our full identity.

Because God loves you, He wants to cultivate Himself in you. Each one of us is uniquely created—when God made you, He broke that mold! Think of it: None of us are alike, and yet, each one of us is created in His image. What an amazing illustration of the unlimited magnificence of God. Consider His mastery in the snowflake.

According to Wonderopolis,[4] "Scientists estimate the chances of two snowflakes being exactly alike are about 1 in

1 million trillion (that's a 1 followed by 18 zeros). Meteorologists think that there are 1 trillion, trillion, trillion (a 1 with 36 zeros!) different types of snowflakes...The temperature of the cloud it forms in determines the shape of an ice crystal. Likewise, the amount of moisture in the cloud determines the size of the ice crystal. More moisture will create a bigger crystal. When several ice crystals stick together, they form a snowflake. As snowflakes tumble through the air, swirling and spiraling, they each take a different path to the ground. Each snowflake falls and floats through clouds with different temperatures and moisture levels, which shape each snowflake in a unique way. Even though two snowflakes may form in the same cloud, their different journeys to the ground will affect their shape and size, giving each snowflake its own unique identity."

The purpose of a Life Season is to allow God to fashion us into the splendor of His likeness, by "tumbling, swirling, and spiraling" us through specific time-and-space conditions, circumstances, and activities. And, the "secret sauce" that enables us to attain our ultimate identity in Him is not *what* we experience, but *how* we experience it!

How we process the conditions, circumstances, and activities of our life will have a direct and dynamic impact on our attitudes, our behaviors, our perspectives, our words, our relationships, and our legacies!

How we process the conditions, circumstances, and activities of our life will have a direct and dynamic impact on our attitudes, our behaviors, our perspectives, our words, our relationships, and our legacies!

God is not chaotic, erratic, vague, nor indifferent regarding the details of your life. He does nothing by chance, coincidence, or luck. God is the Precise and Perfect Designer of your life. He is not forgetful nor indifferent to any aspect of your life. Consider the words of Psalm 37:23 (NLT): "The Lord directs the steps of the godly. He delights in every detail of their lives."

In Psalm 139:13-18 (NLT), David further articulated God's intimate involvement with every detail of your life — "*You made all the delicate, inner parts of my body and knit me together in my mother's womb. Thank You for making me so wonderfully complex! Your workmanship is marvelous—how well I know it. You watched me as I was being formed in utter seclusion, as I was woven together in the dark of the womb. You saw me before I was born. Every day of my life was recorded in Your book. Every moment was laid out before a single day had passed. How precious are Your thoughts about me, O God. They cannot be numbered! I can't even count them; they outnumber the grains of sand! And when I wake up, You are still with me!*"

God created YOU! You are not a mistake, and you are not just a single datum in the collection of humanity! You were born for a reason, and your unique Life Seasons will transform you into harmony with that purpose. Those seasons will also release the fragrance of His Presence from you as you walk through His earth!

We do not experience even one time-and-space condition, circumstance, or activity that is outside His divine jurisdiction! God, and God alone, oversees everything in the universe. He uniquely designed the transition of light to darkness and darkness back to light. He purposely fashioned the mystical transformation of a caterpillar into a butterfly. He appoints particular things to particular times, and He does it meticulously and with excellence. If we allow circumstances to be an excuse for not finding God's secrets in those appointed seasons, we can miss a treasure of enrichment that He has provided for us. And, instead of finding exhilaration, we can become exhausted by stress. It doesn't matter if we see it or not, know it or not, believe it or not. We can discover His purpose *in* every Life Season and successfully possess His purpose *through* every season!

Each and every Life Season has a definite start and stop to it. The secret is to discern each season's shift, and embrace the progression from one season to another. A fruit tree can have a great year of bearing fruit. But, no matter how great that season was, the tree has to be pruned. Pruning may close a past season, but it also represents the preparation for the next season. As hard as I have tried, I've never been able to forbid the enjoyable seasons from leaving me, and I could never prevent the difficult seasons from finding me.

As hard as I have tried, I've never been able to forbid the enjoyable seasons from leaving me, and I could never prevent the difficult seasons from finding me.

WHY JACOB?

Somewhere during my awakening to God's design and application of seasons in our lives, I discovered Jacob. As a major Bible character, he had been hidden in plain sight throughout all my life. I'm sure I first met him in Sunday School. But, I didn't really get to know Jacob until I saw myself in him. That's when I realized he and I shared certain strengths, weaknesses, rejections, bruises, insults, and losses. As I saw that God dealt with me much as He did with Jacob, I leaned into him almost as one of my ancestors. Which, of course, he is! If Abraham is the father of all who believe, then his grandson is certainly one of my relatives.

Through getting to know my great-great-great...grandfather, Jacob, I began studying him. Somewhere in that increased relationship with him is when I saw that he too passed through seasons of God's maturation process. In the Bible, God is frequently called the "God of Abraham, Isaac, and Jacob." All three were great patriarchs of God's promise to His people. But Genesis devotes more space to Jacob than anyone else. That is not because he was a paragon of piety. He wasn't. In fact, our great patriarch's name meant "Heel Catcher." And for good reason: At birth, he grabbed the heel of his twin brother, Esau, in an apparent reach to be born first. But, at death, Jacob was known as "Israel"—one who will rule as God—and became the namesake for a nation.

Now consider the life that unfurled between his "heel catcher" days and his ultimate service as one of God's rulers upon the earth. True to his supplanting nature, Jacob tricked his father, Isaac, into giving him the first-born blessing by masquerading as Esau. Then, reaping what he had sown, Jacob was deceived by his father-in-law, Laban, when he wanted to marry Rachel. Laban forced Jacob to work a total of 14 years just to get her. And, because he manipulated the reproduction of Laban's sheep so he would prosper, Laban accused him of theft. Then, while wrestling with an angel, Jacob dislocated his hip.

Each Life Season holds a treasure that awaits our discovery

Throughout his life, Jacob was emotional, moody, and walked through times of insecurity and confusion. He felt anxiety, pain, and fear, and was even traumatized by pangs of depression. In reading about his life, it became clear that Jacob was just like me and all of my spiritual family! That's when I saw Jacob's life reflected the Life Seasons that we all pass through.

Every one of us is *in, going into,* or *coming out* of a Life Season. They may be linear, simultaneous, sequential, or cyclical. And any Life Season can disorient us about the purpose or progression of that season in our life. Without milestones, we can lose perspective of where we are, and things can become blurry. Are we on target with our life? Are we even on the right road to our destiny? Without a proper understanding of each season, it is easy to become disillusioned and one-dimensional about the entire journey. And, we can miss the unique "gem" of the very season we may find ourselves in. Every Life Season holds a treasure that awaits our discovery!

Others may see the name, sequence, and description of seasons differently from what I will describe in this book. That's fine; God's family is diverse. But, I see life's seasons as divided into two categories, "calling" and "character."

I see the calling seasons as the ones God uses to cultivate our mission (including our vocation and our sense of life-purpose), building us into greater alignment and conformity with His purpose. Those seasons hold unique features, but correlate with each other, as they reflect specific and progressive segments of our purpose. As I see the first three calling seasons—Preparation, Productivity, and Transition—they can be singular or cyclical, as they can be repeated throughout our life journey. The fourth calling season, Impartation, represents the finale of our purpose on earth.

Our character seasons—Despair, Famine, and Refreshing—are those times when God works on our internal nature (our integrity, honor, moral fiber, discipline, ethics, etc.), conforming us into His image. Those seasons also have unique features, but can occur in any or all of our calling seasons. They can appear once or many times in life. Character seasons focus on the attributes of our heart.

LIFE SEASONS

CALLING	CHARACTER
Preparation	Despair
Productivity	Famine
Transition	Refreshing
Impartation	

Just remember, as you read about the seven seasons in the coming chapters, the specific titles or sequences do not represent the true value of the message. What matters is God's transforming power. May you truly discover your treasures and persevere for the joy of your ultimate identity in God.

The next chapter will examine the Season of Preparation. The chapter draws from my own life; after all, I know it very well! But, if you survey your life, I'm sure you will see the same dynamics, themes, and moments in your life. Collectively they reveal the great detail of our Father's love and planning for each of us.

CHAPTER THREE

THE SEASON OF PREPARATION

According to Genesis 25:22,23, the twins, Jacob and Esau, fought in their mother's womb. But, when their mother, Rebekah, asked the Lord why her children were fighting before they were even born, God told her the issue was more than sibling rivalry. Two nations were fighting in her womb.

Naturally, that conflict endured throughout their childhood and young adult years. Finally, when they were adults, the fighting became so intense that Jacob had to flee for his life. Rebekah told Jacob to go stay with her brother Laban in Haran for a few days.

Those "few days" turned into a long-term job. Jacob served Laban for 14 years and married both of Laban's daughters, Leah and Rachel. It could have been only natural for Jacob to think he was working for Uncle Laban because of his past sibling trouble. But, it was during the time with Laban that God prepared him for his future, the birth of his sons. More accurately, the birth of a nation. So, what may have appeared to be a temporary circumstance was the deliberate positioning of God.

WHAT IS THE SEASON OF PREPARATION?

The Season of Preparation is a time of equipping, or retooling, of our thoughts, attitudes, and skills by God. This season makes us ready and positions us to enter the next segment of our purpose.

Do you know your future? Neither do I. But God does. Jeremiah 29:1 (NLT) says, *"For I know the plans I have for you," says the LORD. "They are plans for good and not for disaster, to give you a future and a hope."* Incredibly, the all-powerful, supreme and awesome One actually thinks about each of us, His children, and has carefully crafted His plans for each one's future. God wants to make you ready for *your* future! He directs you *into* your Season of Preparation, and processes you *during* your Season of Preparation, so that you can flourish throughout your entire life.

But, just because you may "have it" doesn't mean you are prepared to "use it!" No one is automatically primed to do what He has purposed us to do. God does not prepare His plan to fit into your life; He prepares your life to fit into His plan.

I came to understand that the Season of Preparation can be *distinct* or *integrative*. Let me explain:

God does not prepare His plan to fit into your life; He prepares your life to fit into His plan.

A *distinct* Season of Preparation is easily recognizable and has definite START and STOP points. The prime focus is on a specific subject that will be pivotal for the future. For example, going to university to study law, accounting, or medicine would be a distinct Season of Preparation, as it gets you ready to be an attorney, accountant, or doctor.

An *integrative* Season of Preparation can be incorporated and concurrent with another season. It is not the prime focus of that season, and sometimes, it might not even be easily recognizable as a Season of Preparation. For example, my first job after high school was working as a purchasing agent for an international mining company. Besides taking courses in purchasing management and accounting for that role, I had to learn to be effective in my communication with employees in other countries. My prime focus was to be a purchasing agent, but God was actually preparing me for my future as founder and CEO of a global corporation—CCLI.

You may be fine for where you've come from, and you may be fine for where you are, but you are not fine for where you are going.

I've learned a key principle about the Season of Preparation: You may be fine for where you've come from, and you may be fine for where you are, but you are not fine for where you are going. God has already gone into your tomorrow, He knows what you need when you get there, and He equips your life so you can thrive there. And, because God already knows where He wants you to go, He directly invests into your readiness to get you there.

The Season of Preparation can be a time of equipping, and it can also be a time of retooling. Let's consider both.

EQUIPPING

As with Jacob, we all start life somewhat helpless and useless. During our formative years, information and instructions often inundate and overwhelm us. "Clean your room, pick up your toys, eat your broccoli, go shower, brush your teeth, get dressed..." We are on a rapid growth track—learning how to eat, walk, talk, behave, and be healthy. That is how our equipping unfolds in our life.

To be certain, we experience things that we may not understand. Your Season of Preparation does not rest on your understanding of what you need for your life. It *is* based on God knowing His plans for you. He knows what you need, whether or not you understand it. During the Season of Preparation, God cultivates our abilities, how we *do* things. He has a masterful maturity program, specifically designed to provide life practicalities in us. God has uniquely created certain skills in you, such as building maintenance, cooking, heart surgery, auditing accounts, writing computer programs, or listening to others. The Season of Preparation will bring you into the delight of discovering your skills.

Our outlook *on* life will always be governed by our response *to* life.

During this season, God also cultivates our mind — how we think about things. We learn in, through, and about life by instruction or experience. God fills us with knowledge and then teaches us to apply knowledge appropriately (called "wisdom"). Sometimes, we have to go through the school of hard knocks because we are hard-headed. During the Season of Preparation, God also cultivates our attitude, how we see things. Our outlook *on* life will always be governed by our response *to* life. God allows events to happen in our life so He can develop our vision for our future. Wrong perspectives can distort our clarity of life purpose.

A pessimist sees the worst possibilities. How did he or she get that way? It may be because of the incorrect development of a wonderful gifting—caring! Perhaps somewhere in the past, a pessimist really cared and hoped for something. When that something didn't happen, maybe disappointment and pain became dominant patterns. Instead of learning how to deal with disappointment correctly, perhaps he or she learned to escape care or hope in order to avoid the pain of disappointment.

For example, let's say a pessimist really loves the Seattle Seahawks (yes, my team). But, prior to the game, he says, "The Seahawks will lose." Does the pessimist want the Seahawks to lose? No! He really wants them to win. But, he has not learned how to handle the pain of disappointment. As a result, the way he *sees* things has been altered. A healthy attitude is cultivated by responding correctly to disappointment.

I love a little story that illustrates a proper outlook on life. A dad was teaching his 6-year-old son to play baseball. He showed the boy how to toss the ball in the air and hit it with a bat. So, the son tossed the ball in the air, swung the bat fiercely, and missed.

"Strike one," Dad said.

The son tossed the ball in the air again and swung and missed again.

"Strike two."

After the swing repeated a third time, the dad said, "Strike three."

Naturally, the dad was concerned for how his son might be feeling. But, before he could say anything, his son shouted with great joy, "Wow, Dad! I never knew I was such a great pitcher!"

God delights in preparing your attitude for your future.

RETOOLING

Typically, a Season of Preparation equips you for a Season of Productivity (which we will address in Chapter 5). In addition to that pattern, we sometimes pass through another Season of Preparation that retools us for another Productivity season. In other words, there are times when God takes what you became as was appropriate for one Season of Productivity, and reworks your thoughts, attitudes, and skills so He can realign you to a new time of Productivity. And, sometimes, alteration is more challenging than origination.

When Jacob wrestled with God (Genesis 32:24-32), that encounter changed the way he walked (he limped for the rest of his life), and it transformed his identity from "Jacob" to "Israel." God retooled Jacob from what he was to what he had to be.

Jacob wrestled with God. That encounter changed the way he walked (he limped for the rest of his life), and it transformed his identity from "Jacob" to "Israel." God retooled Jacob from what he was to what he had to be.

Two Scriptures further illustrate retooling. Isaiah 2:4 (NKJV) says, "*...they shall beat their swords into plowshares, and their spears into pruning hooks...*" And Joel 3:10 (NKJV) says, "*Beat your plowshares into swords and your pruning hooks into spears...*" Have you ever tried to plow a field with a sword? Or have you ever tried to go to war with a plow?

The retooling aspect of Preparation is sometimes a very tough thing to accept. We are often creatures of comfort, familiarity, and routine; we don't like our patterns altered. But because God knows our tomorrow, He wants to fashion us for our future.

Sometimes we may go kicking and screaming into our retooling time. I remember such a time in my life. It did not help when a friend told me God was going to give me a new testimony; I was perfectly happy with my *old* testimony!

My dad, who is such an inspiration to me, started his working life as a window washer for skyscrapers. Following that job, he worked as a bus driver for several years. He then became a pastor and has now been in ministry for over five decades. Even though he got his Bible college degree in the 1940s, he continued his passion for learning and received his master's degree when he was in his 70s. During his mid-30s, Dad decided to learn electronics. And, today, in his 90s, Dad still enjoys learning and using all the new computer technology.

That adaptive nature in Dad is largely because he was not afraid to be retooled multiple times for his future. He couldn't, and you probably can't, take the tools from one season into another. That which brought you here won't take you there.

During a speaking engagement in Boise, Idaho, two members of my host church invited me to go to the shooting range with them. They were expert marksmen who trained local and national law enforcement and military forces. I was honored to come under their tutelage for a few hours. And, they were very complimentary about my marksmanship!

Sometimes your success in the past can be your obstruction in the future.

But then, I noticed, after the first few successful shots of hitting a long-distance mark with a pistol, I began to hit below the mark in subsequent shots. My trainer said I was experiencing what he called, "beginner's muscle memory syndrome." Although I was aiming at the mark correctly, my body pre-adjusted to the shot's upcoming concussion. A marksman learns to negate and nullify the repercussions of past shots in order to hit the mark with future shots.

Sometimes your success in the past can be your obstruction in the future.

So, no matter how much you have learned or accomplished in the past, God might rework you so that you can move into your future.

THE IMPORTANCE OF REPUTATION

King Solomon said, "A good reputation is more valuable than costly perfume." (NKJV) As shocking as it may sound, your avid devotion to Preparation can be easily decimated by your un-attention to reputation.

In the early 1980s, my favorite hockey team, the Vancouver Canucks, had a very popular player, Tiger Williams. When he was on the ice, the fans came alive with anticipation. He may not have been the most talented player on the team, but he was tough and tenacious, and he made things happen! He could score goals. And, he also broke the National Hockey League record for penalty minutes, leading the league twice in being a "bad boy." Although he spent many minutes in the "sin-bin," he knew how to put the puck into the net. But, Tiger had a reputation for "trouble" and, unfortunately, he would end up in the penalty box many times, even when he was innocent. His "reputation" caused the referees to view him differently from the other players. And, his "reputation" hindered his effectiveness.

WHAT'S THE POINT OF TIGER WILLIAMS' STORY?

Reputation is one of the most crucial components in preparation. The word comes from the Latin "*reputationem,*" which means "consideration, thinking over." Reputation is the image, impression, report, news, or notoriety of who you are. It is the cultural reflection of your *character*. In other words, you are labeled by how people see or experience you.

During the Season of Preparation, not only are you building your thoughts, attitudes, and skills for what you do in life, but you are also forming your distinctiveness. Our integrity, trust, and ethics will determine how people view us and act towards us.

How are you perceived by others? Are you considered trustworthy or undependable? Are you seen as gentle or volatile? Do others view you as caring or intolerant? Those are all views of your reputation. The perception of our image can overshadow the intent of our character. People interpret "who" you are by "how" they perceive you. Your reputation can either facilitate or annihilate the value of who you are. Without a doubt, fixing a skill is a whole lot easier than fixing a reputation!

Even Jesus, the Son of God, experienced the construct of reputation. He was prepared to do His "life purpose," and the Bible says that "*...immediately His fame spread throughout all the region around Galilee.*" (NLT) What was His reputation? He went about doing good — that is how He was known. As wonderful as the Preparation for your life purpose may be, it is your reputation that will serve as a conduit for your success!

The perception of our image can overshadow the intent of our character.

How do you build a good reputation? Here are just a few ways that can help.

First, care for others as much as you care for yourself. It's easy to get caught up in self-promotion, self-gain, and self-interest. But, these "self" issues inadvertently convey impressions of devaluing others. And, sadly, the "self" thing has been one of the very roots of demise in contemporary culture. Theodore Roosevelt has been attributed as saying, "*People don't care how much you know until they know how much you care.*" Genuine care demonstrates a heart of love and compassion for others. Genuine care imparts value to others. Genuine care develops value in others and when a person feels valued, they will allow themselves to be influenced by you.

Second, be fair. People want to know that your character scale is not imbalanced or false. People want to know that you will engage with them impartially and honestly. People want to feel that you interact with them without prejudice or favoritism. Fairness includes respecting people's differences and listening without bias. Quite frankly, that's hard! I'm a person who wants to have everybody be happy. But I soon realized that I can't please all the people all the time. Fairness is not something that makes people happy. Life isn't fair! Fairness is not a scheme, it is a foundation. Fairness will convey a character of not being deceitful. When you are being fair, you are able to walk and talk in truthfulness. There will be no need to expend energy trying to cover up hidden agendas!

Third, look in a mirror and watch yourself talk. As silly as this may sound, you need to see your appearance when you interact with others. I was shocked the first time I watched myself speak — I looked so stern. Your countenance is a window to your heart. People form a view of your heart by how you look at them. I learned to practice speaking in front of a mirror so I could make sure my countenance conveyed my content. I recommend it. Do you make eye contact when you speak? Do you appear as engaging, warm, friendly? Can others see a sparkle in your eyes? These are very practical body language tools that can help build a good reputation.

Fourth, monitor your mouth. Oh, how I have often wished I could issue a recall of words that were unfitly spoken! The Apostle James spoke deep truth when he wrote, "*A word out of your mouth may seem of no account, but it can accomplish nearly anything—or destroy it! It only takes a spark, remember, to set off a forest fire. A careless or wrongly placed word out of your mouth can do that. By our speech we can ruin the world, turn harmony to chaos, throw mud on a reputation, send the whole world up in smoke and go up in smoke with it, smoke right from the pit of hell."* (MSG) The words you speak will build or destroy, injure or heal, bless or curse, encourage or discourage. And, as a major part of reputation, you will become known by the words you speak.

Finally, keep your word! This will cultivate and convey dependability to others. Trust me; that will help your reputation! I know that the pace of modern life makes it easy to get over-scheduled. I remember many times when Donna asked what time I'd be home for dinner. And, I also remember often showing up 30 minutes to an hour late. I was building a reputation of unreliability with my own wife! Thankfully, she has forgiven me! Keeping your word conveys how you value your relationship with others. Even your spouse! Doing what you promised creates a reputation of certainty and reliability. Build it at home first.

There was a man in the Bible who experienced great personal increase — Jabez. And, Jabez had a positive reputation — he was more honorable than his brothers. One day, Jabez prayed to God, *"Oh that you would bless me indeed and enlarge my border, and that Your hand might be with me, and that You would keep me from harm that it may not pain me."* (NASB) And, the Bible says that God granted him what he requested. I love what the commentary, Jamieson-Fausset-Brown, states about this Scripture — *"Jabez was, as many think, the son of Coz, or Kenaz, and is here eulogized for his sincere and fervent piety, as well, perhaps, as for some public and patriotic works which he performed. The Jewish writers affirm that he was an eminent doctor in the law, whose reputation drew so many scribes around him that a town was called by his name..."*[5] Jabez's reputation allowed him to influence many scribes, and they named a town after him as a result! Jabez's reputation brought him favor!

The Season of Preparation cultivates your integrity, trust, and ethics. Reputation conveys those personal dimensions of character to others. Pay attention to your reputation.

MY SEASON OF PREPARATION

I need to tell you my story. I do so only because it is the story I know best. I believe it is relevant for every reader because, when I look back at my pathway, I am amazed to see how God put all those little things together. I now see reflections of how He works with all His children.

In my early years, I did not understand that certain details in my life were preparing me for my future with CCLI. Of course, I didn't; the company didn't exist then.

For example, as a 9th grader, I impulsively chose typing as a class elective. Almost immediately, I thought, "Stupid! What were you thinking?" I could have selected band or sports; both would have been more enjoyable. How was I to know then that my typing skills would make me proficient on a computer keyboard in my future at CCLI?

In college, I took courses in accounting, economics, and law, for what I thought would be a career with a large mining company. The Lord derailed that plan very early. But those courses become an essential foundation for my career.

In 1976, I received a certificate of theology from Glad Tidings Bible School. My wife, Donna, and I then moved to Bellingham, Washington, where I became an associate pastor. My biblical grounding and pastoral work would later enable me to exercise a pastoral heart for CCLI.

In 1977, I became the Western Canada Sales Manager for Praise Records and sold gospel music to bookstores. Later that year, I traveled across Canada with Bill Gaither, one of the most prominent songwriters of 20th Century Christian music, and managed the product sales at his concerts. That work in distribution and management gave me industry insights that proved essential for my CCLI career.

In 1970, at 19 years old, I had the great privilege of meeting the great composer and recording artist, Andraé Crouch. Of course, his catalog of compositions is, and always will be, a great gift to churches around the world. And I received so much from him at that level. But, even more, our hearts bonded in brotherhood—backstage, in hotels and restaurants, in our homes, our churches, and vacationing together. We, often with his twin sister Sandra, talked long and deep about our passion for Christ in song (many of those conversations occurred over Ululani's Hawaiian Shaved Ice treats in Maui). Our friendship gave me the sensitivity I needed in relating to artists and songwriters.

Finally, it's vitally important to know that God wants you to be who He has called *you* to be. You can waste a lot of time, money, and effort trying to look like someone or something else. But, that's like trying to paint a cow yellow and teach it to quack and waddle. Go ahead, but it will always be a cow. Trust God to prepare and equip you for your life purpose. His transforming power is the only thing that will enable you to achieve your calling.

The Season of Preparation is your "Get Ready" moment for you to become *you*!

CHAPTER FOUR

THE SEASON OF DESPAIR

Scripture Reference: Genesis 34:1,2,7,30; Genesis 35:19,20,22,29; Genesis 37:3,33-35

Jacob knew God's presence, favor, promises, and blessings. And, he was productive and prosperous as He listened to God and followed His instructions. Yet, Jacob met catastrophic circumstances in his life. He had to journey through the anguish of the Season of Despair.

His daughter, Dinah, was raped. His two sons, Simeon and Levi, became murderers and thieves. His dear wife, Rachel, died. His son, Reuben, committed a sex crime with his concubine. Then, Jacob's father, Isaac, died. Finally, Jacob was told that Joseph, the son he loved the most, had been killed.

WHAT IS THE SEASON OF DESPAIR?

An overwhelming sequence of events slammed into Jacob's world. Staggering in the tumult of tragedy, Jacob tore his clothes, put on sackcloth, mourned, wept profusely, and refused to be comforted. Jacob was caught in the full-throttle grip of a Season of Despair.

Despair, the time of intense agony of affliction, a period when your spirit seems to become detached from hope, is the first of what I see as character seasons. Those seasons set the stage for God to forge character within our frame. And, in His great wisdom, He knows despair works something into people that cannot be attained any other way.

When you are helpless, you feel unable to do anything about a situation. But, when you are hopeless, you feel unable and unwilling to even continue in a situation. Despair tries to persuade you that hope doesn't exist.

Despair is a grueling season. Frankly, I don't want to write about it. I don't want to think about it. I don't even want to acknowledge that it is one of His seasons! How do you articulate the unexplainable, unimaginable, and unbearable pain of that harrowing season? That is the season that cuts through life's joys and rewards; it focuses its fury on our very soul. It hurts; it really hurts.

Everyone passes through things that make them feel helpless. But, there is a difference between being *helpless* and being *hopeless*. When you are helpless, you feel unable to do anything about a situation. But, when you are hopeless, you feel unable and unwilling to even continue in a situation. Despair tries to persuade you that hope doesn't exist.

David described Despair very well in Psalms 55:4-8: "*My heart is in anguish within me, and the terrors of death have fallen upon me. Fear and trembling come upon me, And horror has overwhelmed me. I said, 'Oh, that I had wings like a dove! I would fly away and be at rest. Behold, I would wander far away, I would lodge in the wilderness. Selah. I would hasten to my place of refuge from the stormy wind and tempest."* (NASB)

David wrote of "horror" (intense emotion of fear, dread, and dismay) overwhelming his entire existence. That was the same word Job used to describe the Despair in his own flesh (Job 21:6).

A series of events that come crashing in like a tidal wave often marks a Season of Despair. And, the blessed ordinariness of life can suddenly plunge into the drowning suffocation of Despair.

MY SEASON OF DESPAIR

Our youngest son, Dryden, was a big surprise, as he was born 17 years after Donna's tubal ligation. Obviously, God had other plans, and Dryden filled our hearts with joy on his arrival. "Dry" has always loved football. He set his heart on pursuing football in college. With his brilliant football mind, he hoped to become a football coach. But, sadly, his senior high school year inflicted significant football injuries on our son—knees, shoulders, concussions, ligament strains, and muscle tears.

In December 2014, Dry was playing defensive tackle in the State 2A Football Semi-Finals. In his final play, he re-injured his knee and suffered a serious concussion (the last of several concussions he had throughout the season). In January, he slipped going up the stairs. Another concussion. But, this time, we saw clearly that something was wrong.

After further testing, the doctors discovered he was suffering from "Repetitive Head Injury Syndrome," meaning multiple concussions. Dryden had a loss of long-term memory, as well as vision, balance, and speech trauma. In February 2015, our son began his journey of weekly sessions of occupational and neurological therapy. Every week, for the next 18 months, my wife would take Dryden to his sessions. It was agonizing to see him struggle doing "simple" things. Dryden could no longer remember his early years with his grandparents. Christmases, vacations, family time - they were all a blank wall. It was grueling to see him take one step forward, two steps back, three steps forward, one step back, as he struggled to put "Humpty Dumpty" back together. Our "baby boy" was hurt; naturally, it was excruciating to watch our special gift struggle through the rehabilitation process.

> **My spirit shuddered at the news; Rod was given six months to live. I flashed back to my dear sister's journey with cancer.**

As painful as Dryden's struggle was, this was only the beginning of our entry into our Season of Despair. On Tuesday, March 4, 2014, I received a frantic call from my brother's wife. Something was seriously wrong with Rod. I ran across the street to their house and found him in an incoherent state of confusion. We rushed him to the ER, where they administered several tests. They found some type of growth in his brain. The next day, the doctors performed more tests and conducted a biopsy. I was not prepared for the results; Rod had a Grade 4 glioblastoma multiforme brain tumor. It was inoperable; there was nothing they could do.

My spirit shuddered at the news; they gave Rod six months to live. I flashed back to my dear sister's journey with cancer.

Rod and I were inseparable, joined at the heart. As one of my CCLI executives, he and I had the incredible joy of working side by side for 22 years. We cared deeply for the same things, and we always spent time together, cheering for our favorite teams, playing our favorite sports, and loving the same foods. Rod and I dreamed our hopes out loud together. Others called us "the sons of thunder." We really loved each other. We. Were. Inseparable.

"Oh God, not Rod."

Rod's wife asked me to take the lead in this battle. Networks of believers around the world prayed for him. Finally, with his doctor admitting that medicine held no treatment or hope, we also decided to explore a three-month alternative treatment for Rod in Los Angeles.

As we waged that battle for Rod's life, in early April 2014, we received a phone call from Donna's dad. He had been diagnosed with stage four pancreatic cancer. Doctors gave our beloved Dad Kirkpatrick two months to live.

Dad and Mom Kirkpatrick had been missionaries in Taiwan and Malaysia for over 17 years and then pastored a church in Bellingham, Washington, for another 20 years. Donna and I joined them there as associate pastors and, for 7 years, we were honored to work by their side in ministry. Being in ministry with Dad Kirkpatrick was one of the highest privileges of my life. Besides looking like Billy Graham, he was fun-loving, caring, and one of the most highly skilled people I have ever known. We were a close family, doing holidays, vacations -and Maui- together! Dad Kirkpatrick poured his heart into my life, and I was the recipient of his mentoring. He was such a joy.

"Oh God, not Dad Kirkpatrick."

Over the next seven weeks, we traveled to Canada to be with Dad and Mom Kirkpatrick as much as we could. On May 31 as we gathered around his bedside, Dad Kirkpatrick slipped through his life veil to the other side of eternity.

We spent the summer of 2014 in the intense turmoil of long-distance care-taking. Donna took several trips up to Canada to be with her ailing mother, who was rushed to the hospital several times for medical support. And, I took several trips down to LA to be with my brother. In September, Rod's alternative treatment came to an end. It was time for us all to go back home to Portland; he wanted to spend his remaining time with his family and friends. Sadly, Rod's wife and family chose to stay in LA, and not bring Rod home. So, for several months, our family experienced the horror of disconnection, tearing, and relational rupture.

On January 3, 2015, I received a call from Sandra Crouch, twin sister of Andraé Crouch. She was distraught; Andraé had just gone into cardiac arrest and was being rushed to the hospital. He was placed on life support, and people all around the world began to pray. Andraé was my best friend in the world of gospel music. We had been friends for 45 years; he was the "godfather" to our firstborn child. In fact, when the doctor told us that our baby would probably not survive pregnancy, and if she did, she wouldn't survive birth, it was Andraé who ministered to us. He had just written a new song—"Through It All"—and began to sing it at a Seattle church concert in October 1974. He stopped half-way through the song and said, "Donna, I believe Jesus just touched you right now." He was right. Six months later, our precious daughter, Dyane Gem, invaded our life, screaming and healthy!

"Oh God, not Andraé."

On Thursday, January 8, 2015, Sandra called me and said that Andraé's condition was deteriorating. I immediately hopped on a plane for LA and got to the hospital. Thirty minutes too late. Andraé had passed away.

On the evening of February 26, we received a phone call from Mom Kirkpatrick's doctor in Canada; Mom was rushed to the hospital, and the doctor said she only had a few hours left. Being too far away to make it in time, the doctor put the phone to Mom's ear. Through our tears, we expressed our love and told her goodbye.

Besides being an amazing mother-in-law, she was part of the Latter Rain Revival in North Battleford, Saskatchewan, which became the fountainhead of a great river of the Holy Spirit that flowed around the world. Mom Kirkpatrick was one of the first women ordained by that movement. She had a driving passion for the presence of the Lord, and her passion was contagious.

"Oh God, not Mom Kirkpatrick."

But, in the early hours of February 27, Mom Kirkpatrick also passed away.

Our battle for Rod's life continued. Every month, I flew to LA just to have some precious time with my brother. Brain cancer is worse than atrocious, and my heart wrenched as my "bro" became engulfed in the undignified suffocation of this disease. By May, even though Rod had now become less responsive, his eyes lit up when he saw me. He wrapped his arms around me, began to sob, and wouldn't let go. At the end of June, when my parents and I visited Rod, he could no longer respond. This once tall, strong, handsome, fun-loving, godly man had been reduced to a lifeless state of unconsciousness.

On the afternoon of July 13, I received a phone call from Rod's son; my brother's life was shutting down. With the phone placed by his ear, I told my bro of my deep love for him. Then I released him to God. As I said those words, Rod took his final breath, and heaven welcomed him home.

Two days after we had buried my brother, Donna received a phone call from her sister. She had just been diagnosed with breast cancer and was beginning chemotherapy immediately.

IS. THERE. NO. END. TO. THIS???

The Season of Despair is agonizing for anyone; it certainly was for me. Hurricanes and fires are also agonizing. But, go back to an area 10 years after it was devastated by one. You won't see a wrecked landscape; you will see renewal. Pain, severity, and even death are all part of God's majesty and wisdom. They bring renewal if we embrace them.

Pain, severity, and even death are all part of God's majesty and wisdom. They bring renewal if we embrace them.

And, there is another side to this great mystery. The Season of Despair can bring behavior disorders, fatigue, sleeplessness, depression, personality alterations, psychiatric disarray, relational chaos, mood imbalances, physical deterioration, and spiritual destitution. If left unattended or mishandled, the consequences of despair can be fatal.

That's because self-preservation is inherent; it is an instinct that lives within each one of us. As such, we think that losing our life is the worst thing that could happen. But, Despair breeds within us something far worse than losing our life. It can make us lose our reason for living. And, its havoc can leave people reeling with the unanswerable questions — "Why did God allow this to happen? Why

Despair breeds within us something far worse than losing our life. It can make us lose our reason for living.

did He not stop this? Why did He not heal?" The absence of reason for these episodes of Despair can sow the seeds of anger, resentment, and bitterness against God. "God must not like me. God must be punishing me. God, do you even exist???" — these thoughts flooded my mind.

THE THINGS I *THINK* I LEARNED IN MY SEASON OF DESPAIR

In my own time of Despair, and in helping others through that season, I've learned that Despair can separate people from the frames of reference that help them navigate through life. However, what people often believe will kill them are the very events that God uses to cultivate His character within them.

I cannot say that I know everything that God cultivated in me during that season. But, three keys helped me endure:

1. **The Sovereignty of God**

   First, I realized I needed to find and embrace a clarity and clarification of The Sovereignty of God. God. Is. Sovereign! I know well-meaning friends utter those words to those in Despair; but we often hear them as more religious than helpful. Still, it is a powerful truth. The word "*sovereign*" comes from two Latin words, *superans regnum*. Simplified, this means "above/over the highest kingdom." God's thoughts are nothing like my thoughts; they are immeasurably superior to my highest level of understanding. And, God's ways boundlessly surpass anything I could imagine; they transcend any degree of my intellectual brilliance. God is Sovereign!

> Not one thing that I passed through had any bearing on God's omnipotence.

During my Season of Despair, I learned that my circumstance does not govern God's all-powerful ability. Nor does my circumstance disprove His supremacy. Not one thing that I passed through had any bearing on God's omnipotence. In fact, I am not even a citizen of this temporary earthly environment. My good friend Jack Louman often quoted Teilhard de Chardin, "*I am not a human being having a temporary spiritual experience, I am a spiritual being having a temporary human experience!*" Through Jesus Christ, my real being now dwells in a kingdom that is far greater than my temporary existence. And that is where I can find my full delight.

Peace is not a solution; it is a position, in God's sovereignty!

Another friend, Jim Van Hook, was a key executive in the Christian music industry. In the mid-1990s, Jim faced a battle with cancer. At a publishers meeting, Jim shared how he was feeling about his situation. Instead of expressing fear and worry, Jim acknowledged the uphill climb he was facing. He told us he was at peace. Jim then quoted the following hymn — *My Faith Hath Found A Resting Place*:

My faith hath found a resting place, not in device or creed;
I trust the ever living One, His wounds for me shall plead.
Enough for me that Jesus saves, this ends my fear and doubt;
A sinful soul I come to Him, He'll never cast me out.
I need no other argument, I need no other plea,
It is enough that Jesus died, and that He died for me. (Eliza E. Hewitt, 1891 Public Domain)

In my despair, I discovered a "secret." Peace is not a solution; it is a position in God's sovereignty! God's promise is not that He will solve everything according to my expectation. He promises that He will keep me in "perfect peace" (Isaiah 26:3). In His sovereignty, my eternal nature and destiny are completely and safely undisturbed!

2. The Algorithm of Trust

Once I understood and positioned myself in the *sovereignty of God,* I then had to make a decision, "I will *trust* Him." Our understanding of the word "trust" can be misleading. We typically think of trust as reliance on someone, based on what that person has *done,* his or her track record of past performance. However, in my Season of Despair, I couldn't even comprehend, let alone value, all that God *has done*. But, I learned that trusting Him isn't based upon *what He has done*; it is based upon *who He is*!

That's why it is essential to understand the algorithm of trust found in Proverbs 3:5—"*Trust in the Lord with all your heart, and lean not on your own understanding.*" (NIV)

> Trust is not about the outcome; it's about the outlook.

First, the word "*and*" is a conjunction, connecting two elements in a statement so that it can be complete. To "*trust the Lord with all your heart,*" you must also "*lean not on your own understanding.*" Doing one without the other doesn't work. And, during the Season of Despair, the enemy will manipulate this conjunction incessantly.

Second, the word "*not*" means the activation of one element requires the elimination of the other element. So, in Proverbs 3:5, we have two choices. "*Trust in the Lord with all your heart, and lean* not *on your own understanding.*" Or, "*Trust* not *in the Lord with all your heart, and lean on your own understanding.*" You can't do both. You must cancel your trust in the Lord *or* your dependency on your own understanding.

> The *weapon of thankfulness* is not being grateful *for* the Despair, it is being grateful *in* the Despair.

During the Season of Despair, it is normal to equate trust with outcome—*if* God rescues me, I'll trust Him. But, we forget that Despair is a character season where God cultivates Himself in us! He is right there in your Despair. Trust is not about the outcome; it's about the outlook.

3. The Weapon of Thankfulness

As I persisted during my time of Despair, I became active with the weapon of thankfulness. Yes, thankfulness is a weapon. When I lost my sister to cancer, the enemy robbed me of this valuable battle gear. In the crushing torrent of my agony, I had lost "the secret"—expressing my gratefulness to God. Because I kept saying I *couldn't* thank God during that agony, I carelessly fueled the firestorm of my sorrow. Without a doubt, the vehemence of your Season of Despair can obscure, and even obliterate, the truth of God's great love for you. And, being uncertain about God's love for you only exposes you to the savage storms of anger, resentment, bitterness, hate, disappointment, discouragement, and depression.

Ingratitude is hallucinogenic; it makes you think God is cruel, uncaring, unloving, vengeful, abhorrent, abominable, even non-existent. In Romans 1:21-32, the Apostle Paul expresses the devastating aftermath of ungratefulness — "*Yes, they knew God, but they wouldn't worship Him as God or even give Him thanks. And they began to think up foolish ideas of what God was like. As a result, their minds became dark and confused. Claiming to be wise, they instead became utter fools…So God abandoned them to do whatever shameful things their hearts desired. As a result, they did vile and degrading things with each other's bodies…They traded the truth about God for a lie…Their lives became full of every kind of wickedness, sin, greed, hate, envy, murder, quarreling, deception, malicious behavior, and gossip. They are backstabbers, haters of God, insolent, proud, and boastful…They refuse to understand, break their promises, are heartless, and have no mercy…*" (NLT)

No matter how horrible your Season of Despair may be, ingratitude will make it worse. It is a destructive disease of the soul.

But, why should you be thankful for your Despair?

You can't. I wasn't. The *weapon of thankfulness* is not being grateful *for* the Despair, it is being grateful *in* the Despair. 1 Thessalonians 5:16 says, "***In** everything give thanks; for this is the will of God in Christ Jesus for you.*" (NKJV) Expressing your thankfulness to God *in* your despair positions you in the supremacy of God *through* that season.

So, what is God doing during your time of Despair? What is the reason for the season? I believe God is trying to instill, develop, and strengthen three essential qualities for your life purpose. And, these three qualities can only be engraved on your existence through the Season of Despair.

QUALITY #1 — THE LIFE-WALK OF PERSEVERANCE

During my Despair, God was developing a *life walk of perseverance* in me. Regardless of the challenges, I was committed to walking (yes, sometimes crawling) in my faith path. Almost every day, I confessed a "God-encouragement" found in Ephesians 6:13, and I let its anthem resound through my spirit—"*Having. Done. All. Stand!*"

I discovered that having a heart of faith fortified me with perseverance. It takes courage, great courage, to prevail and to continue in life.

A doctor's recent comment about my high pain threshold made me realize that in order to endure our Seasons of Despair and remain in full engagement with our purpose, we need a high threshold of faith!

When Shammah, one of David's mighty men, faced the Philistines in a heated battle over a lentil field, the Bible says he "*stationed*" himself in the middle of the field, defended it, and killed the Philistines (2 Samuel 23:11-12). No matter the outcome, Shammah would refuse to move. In some modes of ancient warfare, "*stationing*" implied tethering your leg to a stake in the ground, leaving no option for fleeing! Shammah positioned himself in full battle mode. He, having done all, would stand!

You can't go around what God wants you to go through.

In the time of Despair, you may want to run away from everything. You might desperately search for ways to avoid the whole ordeal. That's how I felt, too, until I encountered a word from God: You can't go around what God wants you to go through.

I had exhausted myself trying to avoid the very thing God designed that would strengthen my spirit. And, He also quickened me with the assurance that if He brought me to it, He would bring me through it! In that moment, I knew I had a future.

I also realized I could not persevere through my own efforts. No one has that kind of self-energy. I am weak, but I know Who is strong. As David wrote in Psalm 73:26, "*My flesh and my heart may fail, But God is the strength of my heart and my portion forever.*" (NASB)

To *persevere* is to suffer. Be it physical, emotional, mental or spiritual, everyone who walks with our Lord will walk through suffering. It sounds weird to say that suffering has "benefits." However, in God's hand, suffering refines our priorities, strengthens our endurance, and cultivates compassion for others who face similar crises. Suffering requires dependence on God, and such a dependence reveals His strength in us. From our weakness to His strength, He leads us to His glory!

A *life walk of perseverance* is not a pretense. It is perfectly normal to feel the heat of battle, recognize the severity of the turmoil, and to cry out in the distress. But, along with the distress, the persistent ones will also discover reliance on the absolute reliability of God! David sang it this way (Psalm 18:1-6):

> *How long must I struggle with anguish in my soul, with sorrow in my heart every day? How long will my enemy have the upper hand? Turn and answer me, O LORD my God! Restore the sparkle to my eyes, or I will die. Don't let my enemies gloat, saying, "We have defeated him! Don't let them rejoice at my downfall. But I trust in Your unfailing love. I will rejoice because You have rescued me. I will sing to the LORD because He is good to me.* (NLT)

QUALITY #2 — THE LIFE-WAR OF CONTENDING FOR THE BLESSING

I think part of the purpose of my Season of Despair was that God wanted to teach my hands how to fight. At some point, I saw that God was equipping me in the Battle of Contending for the Blessing. Jacob experienced this same equipping principle when he wrestled with God. Despite being "strenuously urged" to release his grip, Jacob cried out, "*I will not let You go unless you bless me!*" (NKJV) Jacob learned how to hold on and battle for his blessing.

> "I choose to not let my circumstance define my identity!"

In the Season of Despair, you will eventually face the futility of trying to align your circumstance with His goodness and compassion. You can get swallowed up in bewilderment as you try to reconcile the chasm between His power and your desperate situation. In your mind, you are harassed, mocked, and ridiculed by the brutalities of Despair.

> Calamity does not rescind purpose, and Despair is not the absence of His deliverance.

In the heat of the circumstantial insanity, my trust in the Lord was being severely pressed. And, I could have let my trust in the Lord die. But, I had learned to, "having done all, *stand!* So, I stood. And, in that spot, I contended for my blessing and uttered this proclamation—"I choose to not let my circumstance define my identity!"

The hurt was real. The disappointment, discouragement, depression, sickness, abuse, abandonment, brokenness, stress, conflict, pain, uncertainty, pressure...It. Was. All. Real!!! But, I chose not to let these things define my life!

I chose to let my life be defined by Christ. "*For in Him, we live and move and have our being.*" (NKJV) I came to a place of assurance that my identity is in Him!

And, as I contended for my identity in Him, I heard a whisper from heaven, "*When the desire for your destiny outweighs the Despair of your dilemma, only then will you be launched into the fulfillment of all He has called you to!*" Persuasion is potent! It is the elixir for endurance! When you are persuaded that you have a future, you can outlast Despair! In the horror of my circumstances, I saw a firm resolve swell up within me — God still had my future on His heart!

In my Despair, I learned that calamity does not rescind purpose, and Despair is not the absence of His deliverance. God is with you in your Despair! Allow Him to tranquilize your fears and affirm His favor on your *battle of contending for the blessing.*

QUALITY #3 — THE LIFE-DUTY OF GUARDING THE HEART

Life gets cluttered. It distorts priorities and gathers baggage. That's how the compass of life, the *heart*, gets exposed to vanities, delusions, and insanity. That's why we should all pay attention to Solomon's pivotal counsel (in Proverbs 4:23): "*Keep your heart with all diligence, for out of it spring the issues of life.*" (NKJV) Or, as *The Message* says, "*Keep vigilant watch over your heart; that's where life starts.*"

> **"It is written" will be my battle-cry until "it is revealed" becomes my breakthrough.**

I learned that Despair has a way of removing the non-essentials. By that I mean superficiality will get exposed, and *real life* will become your sole focus. The enemy of your soul has an agenda for you during your Season of Despair—he wants to *dishearten* you and disconnect God's purpose from your life. He wants to ravage your heart with hopelessness. But, God wants to fortify you with heart-protecting armor.

During my Season of Despair, one Scripture saturated my heart and carried me to victory. Psalm 27:13-14 contains five ingredients that enabled me to endure.

> *"I would have despaired unless I had believed that I would see the goodness of the LORD in the land of the living. Wait for the LORD; be strong and let your heart take courage; yes, wait for the LORD."* (NASB)

As with David, I would have lost heart and become disconnected from hope, had I not applied those secrets for survival.

- *Believe — I will be convinced that His compassion surpasses my crisis.*
- *See — I will view the temporary from a position of eternity.*
- *Be Strong — I will see and rely on the image of Christ as my Strength, my Rock, my Shield, my Hope of Glory.*
- *Take Courage — I will feed my heart with His Word; "It is written" will be my battle-cry until "it is revealed" becomes my breakthrough.*
- *Wait — I will affix my heart on those expectations that are according to Him.*

Every day, in my distress, I would recite this Scripture, tenaciously clinging to those words with my spiritual fingernails. Above all, I committed to protecting my heart in Him.

Guarding the heart is not a solo act. It needs a close relationship with at least one other person who will walk through the storm with you. That person will not be put off when you process through Despair. He or she should simply listen to you vent. Other times, that friend may need to get in your face and speak the truth with love. As the Bible says, *"Two people are better off than one, for they can help each other succeed. If one person falls, the other can reach out and help…"* (Ecclesiastes 4:9-10 NLT) Along with my wife, several faithful men walked with me through my valley.

And, guarding the heart is a continuous thing, a recurring responsibility that enables you to keep the compass true throughout your life purpose navigation.

Finally, I don't think or hope—I know—that God uses the Season of Despair for our good. But, that doesn't mean we have to like it! Feeling that we must walk through adversity with our religious game face on makes the Season of Despair, or any other season, more difficult. The Lord desires truth ("reality"). And, as His children, we have the freedom to walk before Him in total reality.

I know that God uses the Season of Despair to build something enduring in us because He did that for me. And, His word confirms it. Jesus said, "For everyone will be seasoned with fire, and every sacrifice will be seasoned with salt. Salt *is* good, but if the salt loses its flavor, how will you season it? Have salt in yourselves, and have peace with one another." (Mark 9:49-50, NKJV) God designed our lives to be flavorful. In order to be flavorful, He says we must have the qualities of salt in our lives. How is salt made? You guessed it—heat and fire are used to evaporate the stuff around where salt resides![6] Your Season of Despair is the heat and fire that God uses to flavor your life purpose with Himself.

Despair will make you either *surrender* or *resign*. Surrender is when you take yourself out of the fight. Resignation is when the fight is taken out of you. God uses the Season of Despair to help you *surrender* to, and not *resign* from, His marvelous handiwork. In so doing, you will find life!

CHAPTER FIVE

THE SEASON OF PRODUCTIVITY

Scripture Reference: Genesis 30: 27 — 30, 43

After the Season of Preparation, Jacob stepped into the Season of Productivity. What an exciting time: love, marriage, children, and work, all prospering under God's continuous blessings. Although his childhood didn't seem to predispose him to his new career, Jacob became a farmer.

He quickly discovered some unique ways to multiply his flocks of sheep and goat herds. Showers of abundant blessings fell upon and around Jacob. He walked in a large return on his labors and investments.

WHAT IS THE SEASON OF PRODUCTIVITY?

The Season of Productivity is the time of full engagement in what you are supposed to be doing.

It is a great and delightful season, producing benefits for others, and increasing our personal domain and resources. The season fully utilizes our strength, our "sweet spot." It empowers us and makes us feel alive. The Season of Productivity gives us a great return from our efforts. Naturally, we want the nectar of that season's rewards to last forever.

In retrospect, I was astonished how fast my Season of Productivity as CEO of CCLI went by. It was so much fun! Yes, that time included challenges, setbacks, failures, disappointments, heartache, and discouragement. But, every day in my Season of Productivity was a delight! We worked to cultivate an office atmosphere that was an environment of joy. Naturally, we also worked hard to build relationships with church leaders and within the Christian music industry. But, even more than that, I was committed to serving our employees and making the work fun. And we did! Snowball and whipped cream "fights" in the office, monthly parties and annual picnics, taking the whole company to Disneyland to celebrate a milestone, creating a "Lorinski Cup" golf competition with Geoff Lorenz, owner of one of the oldest Christian music publishing companies — so many wonderful memories!

The Season of Productivity is the time of full engagement in what you are supposed to be doing.

That incredible season saw my creative and strategic skills energized, resulting in unprecedented success for churches, music publishers, and songwriters. Oh how sweet Productivity is! But, no matter how much I wanted it to, the season didn't last forever. No season does.

Although the Season of Productivity often brings personal gain, wealth is not the measurement or proof of our value. Rather, that season marks the increase of our mental, emotional, and spiritual dimensions. It brings a great sense of personal identity, value, and fulfillment. During this time, we know who we are, we see our value, and we feel content. Part of that comes from the appreciation and confirmation that flow from our relationships.

THE INCREASE OF PRODUCTIVITY

During the times of Productivity, our human nature tends to focus on the *results* of our efforts—the great traction, achievements, results, ROI, and accolades. But, God's focus is on the *process* of His purpose in us. He grows Himself in us!

Productivity *is* increase. More specifically, the gauges and indices of Productivity often measure the increases of His life within us.

According to Luke 2:52 (NASB), "Jesus kept increasing in wisdom and stature, and in favor with God and men." The term "kept increasing" reflects advancement, a progressive force, a driving forward. In other words, personal growth is a continual progression of perfection, to be like Him! The wisdom, stature, and favor all measured the increase of His Father's life within Jesus.

"Jesus kept increasing in wisdom and stature, and in favor with God and men." – *Luke 2:52*

What does that mean for us?

1. "Increasing in *wisdom*" represents an expansion of our knowledge, skills, experience, and good judgment. That season develops and polishes our insights. As a result, things which may be difficult and challenging become more intuitive and automatic. For example, tying your

shoes was hard when you were three. But because you increased in wisdom, it soon became a subconscious habit.

We enhance the quality of our existence as we apply what we know. Our decision-making skills get sharpened, sometimes by trial and error; we call that "experience!" As we face challenges, we become "less stupid!" According to a statement usually attributed to Albert Einstein, "*The difference between stupidity and genius is that genius has its limits.*" The increase of wisdom demonstrates the "genius" of good judgment!

2. I see "Increasing in stature" as the time in which He expands our character. We learn integrity, trust, and ethics. In this time, who you *are* eclipses what you *do*.

   Remember, how we conduct ourselves creates a reputation that filters how people view us and, consequently, act or react towards us. But, also remember, even when you uphold integrity, trust, and ethics, some people just won't like you! When people said something negative or erroneous about me, I tried to remind myself—Those who know me, know better, and for those who don't know me, it "don't" matter!

3. Our "Increase in favor with God" brings an expansion of God's favor and blessings. As simple as this may sound, my life "wellness" flourished when I listened to God and obeyed Him!

   At the very beginning of CCLI, the Lord spoke to us through a Scripture quickened to my business partner and dear friend, Victor Anfuso. Deuteronomy 8:17,18 (NLT) says, "*He did all this so you would never say to yourself, 'I have achieved this wealth with my own strength and energy.' Remember the LORD your God. He is the One who gives you power to be successful, in order to fulfill the covenant He confirmed to your ancestors with an oath."* With that word in mind, CCLI established a stewardship creed —*"Revenue is not our objective. Service is our objective, and revenue is the fruit of our service."* The purpose of the Season of Productivity is so we can be facilitators of His blessings and favor. That advances Him in, to, and through others.

4. Through the "increase in favor with man" our life begins to speak to others. Not only did Jacob find favor with God, but he also experienced favor from one who hated him, his sibling rival, Esau. When the increases of favor with man come from the Lord, it will touch some of our one-time enemies.

As the devil ran away from me, I remember thinking, "Hmm, the devil must have realized that I'm not as easy as he thinks I am." Just then, I looked down and saw a huge shadow come up behind me.

In 1988, when we were launching CCLI, I dreamed I walked out into an Old West setting, where I was going to have a duel with the devil. High noon on the dusty main street. I was dressed in my white outfit, while the devil was, of course, dressed in a black Stetson, black shirt, black trousers, black boots, black spurs, and black pistols. As we faced each other, I saw the sneering, mocking disdain in his eyes; I was *nothing* to him but another notch on his gun grip. But, then I saw his eyes change, from contempt, to surprise, to uncertainty, to concern, and then to fear. His shoulders drooped, and he turned and ran away.

As the devil ran away from me, I remember thinking, "Hmm, the devil must have realized that I'm not as easy as he thinks I am." Just then, I looked down and saw a huge shadow come up behind me. Oh, I realized, the devil didn't run because of me; he ran because he saw God behind me. Then I heard God tell me, "Son, when I say duck, you better duck. Because if I have to use my guns, I don't want to blow your head off! Keep. Your. Head. Low." That dream dropped a nugget into my soul that has stayed with me since that night—the more favor I receive, the more humility I need.

Humility is essential. That's because the favor with man opens up three avenues that help us make a difference in people's lives. And all three hold powerful enticements to our pride.

1. We will have opportunities to give *input*. Because of the increase of favor with man, our diligence, steadfastness, experience, and integrity will be more visible. And people will invite our perspective, expertise, and knowledge.

2. We will also have *influence*. We will awaken value in others. But, that comes from how we live more than what we say. When you live out His purpose, it draws others to Him and His ways. That is the essence of influence. It is always filtered through how we live. What you do speaks volumes more than what you say.

3. We will also find new arenas of *impact*. Here's how Laban described Jacob's impact, "*... I have learned by experience that the LORD has blessed me for your sake.*" (Genesis 30:27 NKJV) Just as Jacob's son Joseph impacted Egypt's Pharaoh, when people experience the blessing of God that comes through us, they will invite more of our counsel.

FIVE PITFALLS OF PRODUCTIVITY

Productivity is so full of richness that it makes us all think it is the ultimate of our existence. We naturally want to savor the Season of Productivity as long as possible. But, while we live in that delightful season, it is easy to become drunk with the nectar of personal achievements. That brings some snares which can entrap us and jeopardize His blessings. Having walked through that season, I see five pitfalls:

1. The first is COMPLACENCY. During the Season of Productivity, it is easy to become so enchanted with achievement that we lose awareness of pending dangers. The sweet savor of accomplishments can lull us into a false sense of security. Complacency is not synonymous with contentment. Being content flows from gratitude for all the Lord has done through us. But complacency is a smugness built around pride in our own efforts. That arrogance can cause us to let our guard down. Complacency often causes people to slip from vigilance to indifference. That can be ruinous. Proverbs 1:32 (NASB) captures it so well: "For the waywardness of the naïve shall kill them, and the complacency of fools shall destroy them." Jesus expounded on complacency when he told the story about the rich man, *"And I'll sit back and say to myself, 'My friend, you have enough stored away for years to come. Now take it easy! Eat, drink and be merry.'" But God said to him, "You fool! You will die this very night. Then who will get everything you worked for?"* (Luke 12: 19-20

The tragedy of complacency is that it can rob you of the fruit of your labor, and subsequently steal or demolish your completeness in life.

NKJV) The tragedy of complacency is that it can rob you of the fruit of your labor, and subsequently steal or demolish your completeness in life.

2. The second pitfall, COMPROMISE, tempts us to forsake our values for the pursuit of pleasure. It will distort our perspective about the guidelines and disciplines that helped us succeed in the first place. We begin to justify our digressions. That kind of compromise has destroyed many careers, marriages, and lives. The Bible is full of warnings about the entrapments of compromise. And it also celebrates those who maintain their integrity and refuse to compromise. Psalms 119:1 (NLT) says, "*Joyful are people of integrity...*" *The Message* translates that as, "*You're blessed when you stay on course, walking steadily on the road revealed by GOD.*" Compromise comes when we stop "walking steadily" towards God and what He holds for us.

Your calling helps to get you there, but your character helps to keep you there.

   Compromise is poison to our spiritual health; it can seduce us away from our righteous affections. Fantasy is deceptive — it leads the heart away from being upright in character. Compromise does not satisfy appetite, status, or image! Compromise always brings great risk. When we gamble with God's blessing, life can become a casualty, not a celebration. Remember, your calling helps to get you there, but your character helps to keep you there.

3. The third pitfall is ENTITLEMENT. During the Season of Productivity, it is easy to become persuaded that we deserve special treatment. Because of our culture

of entitlement, we easily forget how fortunate we really are. Everyone has seen privileges as rights rather than His generous blessings.

Entitlement, which is so pervasive in our culture, is the abandonment of gratefulness. Chris Tiegreen said, "Thankfulness is difficult to express when one starts with an attitude of entitlement."[7] This pitfall launches a war within our mind; we can end up believing the government, employers, schools, banks, churches, etc. owe something to us.

> **"Thankfulness is difficult to express when one starts with an attitude of entitlement."**
> **– *Chris Tiegreen***

An attitude of entitlement can cause people to groan and complain about "injustices," or announce that "life is not fair." But, life does not owe us anything; God does not owe us anything! The more we pursue a perceived entitlement to rights, the more deceived we become. James 4:1,2 (MSG) says, "*Where do you think all these appalling wars and quarrels come from? Do you think they just happen? Think again. They come about because you want your own way, and fight for it deep inside yourselves. You lust for what you don't have and are willing to kill to get it. You want what isn't yours and will risk violence to get your hands on it. You wouldn't think of just asking God for it, would you? And why not? Because you know you'd be asking for what you have no right to. You're spoiled children, each wanting your own way.*"

> **Jacob positioned his heart to be a servant, so that he could provide value to others.**

From where I sat in my career, I have seen the spirit of entitlement creep into Christian music. We all—songwriters, artists, and executives—have enjoyed the fellowship of sharing memories of the early years in the music industry. We've all laughed together as artists recalled touring in broken-down VW vans and sleeping on church basement floors. We've recalled in gratitude about when that first hit launched them into a higher orbit of success. We've celebrated together when their album went "gold" and "platinum."

But, I have also seen contracts that included demands for first-class air tickets, limousines, luxury suites, extravagant catering, exorbitant entourage expenses, and unreasonable appearance fees. No one wanted to see them continue to drive in broken-down vans or sleep on floors. But, sometimes a subtle and imperceptible attitude shift can move a person from gratitude to entitlement.

4. The fourth pitfall of INVINCIBILITY can lead us to believe that everything we do is unconquerable and unstoppable. The scent of power can make us act as if we are bulletproof! It can convince a person that everything he or she touches will turn to gold. We begin to think that our repetitive successes immunize us from failure.

   I confess; I experienced the peril of this pitfall.

   Because of CCLI's successful accomplishments, many opportunities opened up for us. In the early 2000s, digital music download services were being launched, and some key Christian music executives encouraged CCLI to provide this resource for churches. So, with unabated confidence in our "track record," we launched a "Christian iTunes®" company, providing only "safe," Judeo-Christian value songs. Our "success pedigree" would surely lead us to another great accomplishment, right?

Wrong!

Our digital content provider dissolved, our marketing was ineffective, and we suffered significant loss. Our intention was good, our assumption wasn't. Every stream thinks it is *the* river. I thought we were unstoppable; we weren't.

Invincibility blocks our ability to hear counsel, receive instruction, see strategically, and enjoy the rewards of success. And, that leads to deception, which invites arrogance. Invincibility causes people to see themselves as higher, better, smarter than everyone else.

5. No season lasts forever. But, the fifth pitfall is PERPETUITY. This attitude seduces people into believing that the season's successes will last forever, that the "sweet spot" will never end. Trust me; it stops. Perpetuity distorts how we view our entire life; it makes us want to memorialize our conquests. We want our identity to last forever, and we begin to think this can be accomplished by constructing monuments that adulate our efforts. As Proverbs 27:24 (NASB) reminds us, "*... riches are not forever, Nor does a crown endure to all generations.*"

   The author of those words, Solomon, King of Israel, knew the depth of that truth. Despite his wisdom, he surrendered to the attitude of perpetuity. He thought those days would never end. However, near the end of his life, an even wiser Solomon acknowledged, in Ecclesiastes 3:1 "To everything, there is a season..."

   Waste is a byproduct of the pitfall of Perpetuity. Those who think the Season of Productivity will never end will tend to misuse time and resources. They should

> read Roman philosopher Seneca's words, "*You live as if you were destined to live forever, no thought of your frailty ever enters your head, of how much time has already gone by you take no heed. You squander time as if you drew from a full and abundant supply, though all the while that day which you bestow on some person or thing is perhaps your last.*"[8]

The Season of Productivity is just that, a season. On this side of Eternity, there is a start and a stop to everything!

THE GUARDIANS OF PRODUCTIVITY

Although Jacob displayed some negative behavior during his Season of Productivity, he also demonstrated two crucial guidelines that helped him to navigate the pitfalls.

First, Jacob had a "heart of service." He positioned his heart to be a servant so that he could provide value to others. He established a seven-year "strategic plan" whereby his focus and dedication to work would ultimately reward him. And, even when there was an obstacle that threatened his plan, he continued with a heart of service for another seven years. Jacob simply got things done by serving. Despite the setbacks, a heart of service will help you navigate towards your destiny.

Second, Jacob had a "heart of love." His love for Rachel was so strong that I'm sure his daily testimony reflected some variation of, "My, how time flies when you're having fun!" Love is a powerful weapon! Remember - your outlook *on* life affects your enjoyment *in* life!

May you thoroughly enjoy and thrive in your Season of Productivity. And, may you know its true purpose in your life through Him Who gives it!

CHAPTER SIX

THE SEASON OF FAMINE

Scripture Reference: Genesis 41:29,30,56,57; Genesis 42:5,6; Genesis 43:1

After God led Jacob to Canaan, he passed through both agony and ecstasy. But, Jacob still knew that God had promised him a great legacy to pass on to his seed. Then, while Jacob was still trying to align his temporary predicament with his life purpose, he and his household were launched full throttle into the Season of Famine. That's when Jacob began to know scarcity. Despite the blessing upon Jacob's life, famine touched every aspect of his existence: his resources, productivity, family, wellness, and future.

> Famine does not reduce any of its ferocity for the wealthy and famous, and it gives no sympathy to the impoverished and underprivileged.

Have you ever felt completely and helplessly engulfed in emptiness? Or, suffocating in a vacuum of forsakenness? If you haven't, you will. Everyone experiences famine.

The Merriam-Webster dictionary defines famine as "*an extreme scarcity of food, a great shortage, starvation.*"[9] Famine is a condition in which your own skill, expertise, talent, and resources cannot produce the necessities for survival. Your accomplishments, accolades, successes, money, and fame cannot protect you from the scourge.

> I felt like the heavens were brass – I couldn't hear God, and I was sure God couldn't (maybe even wouldn't) hear me.

The Season of Famine respects no one. It gives no regard to age, gender, race, or class of society. It does not reduce its ferocity for the rich and famous, and it gives no sympathy to the impoverished. And Famine often seems both permanent and fatal at the same time.

WHAT IS THE SEASON OF FAMINE?

I imagine that Jacob must have asked himself a thousand questions about why he faced such deprivations in his life. After all, he was a faithful and obedient man; he walked with the Lord. But, even in his obedience, Jacob also walked through insufficiency.

The Season of Famine is the time and place in which your heart remains hungry and thirsty, but your mental, emotional, physical, and spiritual resources are dry and barren. You become parched and tapped-out. Life gets reduced to placing one foot in front of the other. All day. Every day.

Some think the season is a "mid-life crisis." So, they buy toys, launch hobbies, or indulge in sensual pleasures as antidotes or escapes. None of that will bring relief; the season is much deeper than that.

A natural famine batters your body. But, a spiritual famine wars against your soul; it tests us through intense emptiness, loneliness, and dejection.

EMPTINESS

This condition provokes a strong sense of deprivation. Life seems to contain nothing. You feel completely empty. All the usual and reliable nourishments seem absent and unattainable. Try as you may, you can find no water, no food, no energy-pack, no secret stash for your soul. Nada.

Emptiness made my soul starve.

In my Season of Famine, I felt an overwhelming sense of depletion, like every ounce of vitality had been sucked out of my being. I was puzzled: Why did I feel so "lifeless"? I felt like the heavens were brass; I couldn't hear God, and I was sure God couldn't (maybe even wouldn't) hear me. My heart felt desolate and barren. I was hungry, empty, running on fumes. Although I remembered all that God had brought me to, and through, I came face to face with a "heart vacancy." I felt like I had lost my vibrancy.

LONELINESS

The Season of Famine also brings a strong sense of isolation; I felt totally separated from others. All the normal enjoyments and strengths of relationships seemed hollow and distant. I felt marooned on an island; I had no boat. I felt an overwhelming sense of alienation. That kind of loneliness can convince you that even God has deserted you. I felt like I had been stabbed with a knife. I felt bewildered in my spiritual exile.

That depth of loneliness is not just seclusion; it feels like total abandonment. Only when you've passed through it can you understand what the Psalmist David groaned in his terrible agony of abandonment in Psalm 22:1-2, "*My God, my God, why have You forsaken me? Far from my deliverance are the words of my groaning. O my God, I cry by day, but You do not answer; and by night, but I have no rest.*" (NASB) I felt cast aside; I couldn't see Him, feel Him, touch Him, or hear Him. My life "radar" could not locate where God was!

I was hit with a double-whammy, as I experienced my Season of Famine in the midst of my Season of Despair. Yes, they are different. In despair, you face external storms that clobber your circumstances. However, in famine, internal storms assault your identity.

I didn't know "up" from "down;" my life stabilizers were not working, and I felt very alone.

My role as CEO of CCLI required much travel, including several international trips annually. On one overnight trip to the UK, I was repeatedly jolted from sleep. Once awake, I was completely disoriented as to where I was and why I was there. It took several minutes of forcing my memory pieces together before I could sort it out.

As we approached London Heathrow, we descended into a thick cloud bank; every dip and roll of the plane created vertigo. In my disorientation and vertigo, and having endured months of Famine, my mind became haunted by this thought—*No one knows who I am or where I am, and no one cares.* I didn't know "up" from "down"; my life stabilizers were not working, and I felt very alone. My spirit had become malnourished and my identity had become obscured.

Throughout my life, I have usually been able to sense God's nearness to me. So, my Season of Famine found me unprepared for the chill of loneliness that came from not sensing His Presence. In fact, I had no assurance of *anyone's* nearness. I felt lost and abandoned.

DEJECTION

In my Season of Famine, I felt completely broken and cast down, deflated. All the normal joy of accomplishment seemed shallow, almost like an illusion. I felt disconnected from the promise and potential of my life. At times, I was flattened by staggering heartbreak. I also felt an overwhelming sense of failure. That was serious; I thought God had failed me. And I became discouraged. Dejection is the depression of our personal value. That season taunted me with an inner voice: *Didn't God say that He would always be with me? Didn't He say that He would never leave me?*

If He said it, why has this happened? Why have I been cut off from Him and others? Why do I feel lost and empty? Why am I alone? Why does no one care?

My sense of dejection felt intimately cruel and callous. It came close to convincing me life held no more value. I felt the future offered no hope.

WHAT IS THE PURPOSE FOR THE SEASON OF FAMINE?

I became convinced that Famine had no value. But, right in the midst of hunger and scarcity, seeds of transformation can sprout.

For me, the Season of Famine cleared out the clutter in my heart. As we travel through life, we can become glutted by our achievements, possessions, and comfort zones. We unwittingly collect memorabilia we consider indispensable. We are life-hoarders, experience junkies. But, as much as we cherish those possessions, they can become roadblocks. Life gets clogged by them.

Let me shoot straight; the Season of Famine is a "*Souloscopy,*" a colonoscopy of the soul! As the Star Wars movie character Yoda might say, "Dread it, you undoubtedly do; undertake it, you unavoidably must."

The Season of Famine is an essential "Souloscopy" – the colonoscopy of the soul.

In case you did not know, a colonoscopy begins with a thorough and effective cleansing of your colon. To achieve that, the doctor prescribes a product that "may cause some slight discomfort." Are you kidding me? That "slight discomfort" brought an incessant, gargantuan, internal detonation; I was afraid to move two feet away from the toilet. But, by the next morning, I was empty of any clutter that might have obstructed my colonoscopy.

And, that emptying is exactly what the Season of Famine does for your life. The acquisitions of the past can clog your internals, impair your spiritual metabolism, and inhibit advancement in the Lord. Famine expedites the removal of those comforts, expectations, and memorabilia that impede your purpose.

THE SEASON OF FAMINE BUILDS ENDURANCE

In May 2018, a science blog in *The Guardian*[10] reported that, regarding speed, "humans are outperformed by almost every animal in the animal kingdom, including the wild donkey, the ostrich, and the elephant." However, the longer the distance, the better humans perform. A study, conducted on the 690 km Yukon Arctic Ultra foot race, discovered some surprising insights about the sympathetic and the parasympathetic wings of the nervous system: "In a relaxed state, parasympathetic (or vagal) tone dominates, while conversely, a state of emergency activates sympathetic pathways, causing the heart rate to increase and blood to be diverted from the gut to skeletal muscles." To simplify, when a person enters a crisis, the body pulls from its own resources to supply the focus of the emergency. But, long-distance survivors learn how to balance a relaxed state of function along with the emergency.

And, so it is in life; the Season of Famine builds your stamina so you can become strong enough for where you are going. Endurance enables a person to survive and thrive through all of life's seasons. Endurance is not *discovered*; it is *developed* through the persistent, repetitious, and habitual exercise of one's faith.

The Apostle Paul wrote to the church at Colossae, "*We also pray that you will be strengthened with all His glorious power so you will have all the endurance and patience you need. May you be filled with joy.*" (Colossians 1:11 NLT) And I like the way *The Message* paraphrases Hebrews 12:1: "Strip down, start running — and never quit! No extra spiritual fat, no parasitic sins."

> Endurance is not *discovered*; it is *developed* through the persistent, repetitious, and habitual exercise of one's faith.

When we go to our summer vacation home, I take full advantage of the resort gym, which is loaded with fitness equipment. On all the non-golf days, I power walk 5 miles and then spend 45 minutes on the fitness equipment. But, when I first start this ordeal, I find myself quickly out of breath during my walk. I must exert every muscle fiber I have just to make it through. Naturally, the first several days abound with incomprehensible groanings and absolute agony. But, I stay the course.

After a while, my breathing becomes more relaxed, and I can add more weights to the equipment.

The Apostle James speaks of endurance this way — *"For you know that when your faith is tested, your endurance has a chance to grow. So let it grow, for when your endurance is fully developed, you will be perfect and complete, needing nothing."* James 1:3-4 NLT

The Season of Famine does the same thing for your life; it tests your faith so that you can build endurance. If you stay the course, you will develop the traits that God has deposited into your heart. And, they will carry you through.

THE SEASON OF FAMINE REVEALS THE SINCERITY OF THE SOUL

The Greek word for sincere, "eilikrinēs," means "judged by sunlight[11]"; the sun reveals it as genuine. The Latin word for "sincere" derives from two words, "sine = without" and "cera = wax." During the age of the Roman Empire, Roman leaders memorialized their feats of victory by commissioning marble sculptures of themselves. The sculptors would endeavor to select perfect marble to accomplish this task. But, occasionally, as he worked, the sculptor would discover flaws in the sculpture. So, he could choose another piece of marble, eating the cost of the defect, or he could cover the flaw with wax and try to deceive the customer.

> That is exactly what the Season of Famine does in your life – it exposes the real you.

Because of that practice, when the sculpture was ready for inspection by the owner, an astute Roman leader would place the sculpture in the sunlight and let any wax melt from the heat of the sun. That is what the Season of Famine does in your life; it exposes the real you. God uses your time of emptiness, loneliness, and dejection to boil the debris from your life. God wants your life to be "without wax," free from any cover-up.

When Frances Jane van Alstyne was a baby, a doctor's mistake left her blind for life. Instead of letting her blindness turn to bitterness, she embraced the lack of sight. As a result, she began to see the value of eternal realities as much higher than the things of earth. At eight years old, she composed this verse:

In the Season of Famine, God can change your focus around from the past to the future.

"Oh, what a happy child I am, although I cannot see!
I am resolved that in this world contented I will be!
How many blessings I enjoy that other people don't!
So weep or sigh because I'm blind, I cannot – nor I won't."[12]

Frances is better known as Fanny Crosby, the composer of approximately 9,000 hymns, including "Blessed Assurance," "To God Be the Glory," "Near the Cross," and "He Hideth My Soul."

Years later, she said, "It seemed intended by the blessed providence of God that I should be blind all my life, and I thank him for the dispensation. If perfect earthly sight were offered me tomorrow, I would not accept it. I might not have sung hymns to the praise of God if I had been distracted by the beautiful and interesting things about me."[13]

The Season of Famine will strip away your personal attachment to life's embellishments. And it will help you savor the real nourishment that fulfills your life purpose.

THE SEASON OF FAMINE PREPARES THE HEART FOR FUTURE ENRICHMENT

2 Kings 7:3-20 tells the story of Syrians besieging the city of Samaria, resulting in severe famine. Four lepers, sitting at the entrance of the city gate, felt the impact of the famine more than most. Because they depended on help from others, and their benefactors had no food, their flow of supply stopped. Knowing they would surely die where they sat, the lepers decided to get up and move; they had nothing to lose. So, they rose up and walked to the Syrian camp, the cause of their famine. When they got there, the Syrians were gone. And, at the very source of their Famine, they found an abundance of food, water, and wealth!

Amid their Famine, those four lepers chose not to focus on the way supplies had arrived in the past. Instead, they decided to find provisions for their future. As He did for them in Famine, God can change your focus around from the past to the future. Perhaps more pointedly, He can help you turn from the way His provision once came to a whole new path of His supply in your life.

Jacob also found that he could not stay where he was. A Season of Famine brought him to the end of his past provision. He too needed to find a new path to his future. That new path took him to Egypt, and his new provision, through his son Joseph. And Joseph saw the sure hand of His God in that process; he said, "*God intended it all for good. He brought me to this position so I could save the lives of many people.*" Genesis 50:20 NLT

Even though you may not sense it, God's Presence is in your Season of Famine.

SURVIVING THE SEASON

I know some readers are asking, "How do I survive my Season of Famine?" The keys I discovered in my own Famine may be helpful to you.

First, clothe yourself with these words from Isaiah 58:11(NKJV) — *"The LORD will guide you continually, and satisfy your soul in drought, and strengthen your bones; you shall be like a watered garden, and like a spring of water, whose waters do not fail."* Even though you may sense nothing, God is always at work in you. He never sleeps and He never slumbers. His delight for your eternal purpose far surpasses your limited assessment of the temporary famine. Trust me; God has not forsaken, forgotten, nor terminated your life.

Second, understand why the Lord brings Famine into the lives of His children. He dictates rest for those parts—you and me—of His great symphony. To do that, we must stay focused on Him.

The British writer John Ruskin captured this truth so well: *"There is no music in a rest, but there is the making of music in it. In our whole life-melody the music is broken off here and there by "rests," and we foolishly think we have come to the end of the tune. God sends a time of forced leisure, sickness, disappointed plans, frustrated efforts, and makes a sudden pause in the choral hymn of our lives, and we lament that our voices must be silent, and our part missing in the music whichever goes up to the ear of the Creator.*

"How does the musician read the rest? See him beat the time with unvarying count, and catch up the next note true and steady, as if no breaking place had come between.

"...Not without design does God write the music of our lives. But be it ours to learn the tune, and not be dismayed at the "rests." They are not to be slurred over nor to be omitted, nor to destroy the melody, nor to change the keynote. If we look up, God Himself will beat the

time for us. With the eye on Him, we shall strike the next note full and clear."[14]

During your Season of Famine, you can frantically count out the beats of nothingness and miss the harmonic mystery of the moment, or you can keep your eyes on the Conductor. He will bring you back into the symphony at exactly the right time. Keep your eyes on Him.

During your Season of Famine, you can frantically count out the beats of nothingness and miss the harmonic mystery of the moment, or you can keep your eyes on the Conductor. He will bring you back into the symphony of your life purpose at exactly the right time.

Third, keep on blessing others. Even in his Season of Famine, Jacob understood this principle: Make a positive difference for others. Even when he had to send his sons back to Egypt to get more food, Jacob made sure they took with them "*some of the best fruits of the land in your vessels and carry down a present for the man — a little balm and a little honey, spices and myrrh, pistachio nuts and almonds.*" (Genesis 43:11, NKJV) Even in Famine, Jacob blessed others with something.

Famine can make you feel you have nothing to give, but you do. And that something can make a difference in somebody's life. Push beyond the focus on survival to contribute to the lives of others.

Andraé Crouch's passing came during my Season of Famine. But Andrae's twin sister, Sandra, asked me to help with the funeral arrangements and the planning for Andrae's Celebration of Life service. The first event was the Sunday morning service at New Christ Memorial Church (where Andraé and Sandra were the pastors). Several dignitaries would be in attendance, and that service would set the tone for an extraordinary week.

Sandra asked me to preach for that service. She didn't know about my Season of Famine. But, I did. And, in my dryness, I did not want to do that. I didn't want the responsibility. But, Sandra was unrelenting; "You are to give a word to the church."

Game. Set. Match. There was no changing her mind; I reluctantly agreed to do that.

I opened my heart to Donna, "Honey, Sandra has me speaking on Sunday, and I have absolutely nothing in my well. I am empty, dry, tapped out. I have nothing!"

And, that's when Donna prayed for me.

The next morning, God opened a repository of His Word in me. Where did *that* come from? Despite my own aridity, I tapped into some of His hidden "honey, spices, and myrrh." He gave me a message for New Christ Memorial. With a big I-told-you-so smile on her face, Sandra said, "You did good, Howard, real good!"

Even in your Season of Famine, you may discover great caches of His Word. Even in Famine, you can make a difference in someone else's "world."

THE WEALTH OF HIS UNFAILING LOVE

The phrase "unfailing love"—implying lovingkindness, mercy, favor, beauty, and goodness—is used 121 times in the New Living Translation of the Bible. God told Moses, "I lavish unfailing love for a thousand generations on those who love Me and obey My commands." (Exodus 20:6, NLT) The Psalmist David declared, "Your unfailing love, O LORD, is as vast as the heavens; your faithfulness reaches beyond the clouds." (Psalm 36:5 NLT) And, the Apostle John said that God's unfailing love and faithfulness came through Jesus Christ. But, in your Season of Famine, those statements may seem unrealistic and diametrically opposed to real life.

When my son, Deryk, was a little child, I asked him, "Do you know how much I love you?"

"How much?"

I then wrapped my arms around him and said, "All the way to the back!" My answer brought a huge grin to his face, and he wrapped his arms around my neck and repeated, "All the way to the back." Ever since that moment, no matter what we have had to experience in life, good and bad, enjoyable or stressful, explainable or unexplainable, "ATW2TB" has become our secret code!

Unfailing love is not the absence of adversity; it is the assurance of advocacy!

How does the Season of Famine affirm His unfailing love? By staying locked onto the course of your purpose! By having faith in your "tomorrow." By trusting your Eternal Guide. He will satisfy your soul in drought.

Donna and I love to go to Cannon Beach on Oregon's beautiful coast for breathers. That beach is long and flat, and waves crash so majestically on the shoreline. One morning I went for a long walk and enjoyed engraving my footprints in the sand. After a few miles, when I headed back to the hotel, I decided to follow my footprints back to the hotel. All went well for a while. But, then I came to a section of the beach where the waves had washed my footprints away. I couldn't use them as a guide for my future. But, then I realized if I could keep my eye on the horizon and stay the course, I would find my way. I just had to keep going. That served as a good reminder to keep singing my search to see, hear, and know the Invisible One!

His unfailing love provides stability in the famine. Our emptiness will never deplete His fullness. Loneliness does not mean His love has wavered, and dejection does not mean He never brought us joy. Unfailing love is not the absence of adversity; it is the assurance of advocacy! God is not stunting your life's purpose; He is building it.

Regardless of your season, you can fortify your purpose with these proclamations:

- *I will wait for Him!*
- *Even though He feels absent, I know He is near!*
- *I will put all my hope in Him!*

No emptiness, loneliness, or dejection can dissipate or invalidate His unfailing love! How much does God love you? ATW2TB!

Stay the course!

CHAPTER SEVEN

THE SEASON OF TRANSITION

Scripture Reference: Genesis 31: 13, 20, 21

In Chapter 4, we saw Jacob in his "sweet spot" season. He was productive, his work prospered, his family grew, and his life flourished. Oh, how sweet it was!

But, then God uprooted him from everything he had worked for and pressed his life through convulsive change. It often seems that just when we learn how to live, everything changes,

The Season of Transition closes the Season of Productivity and takes us into a new one. Transition often brings an awkward, in-between, and neutral zone shift in life's journey.

You already know that change is hard; it hurts. It rarely seems right or fair. But, the Season of Transition doesn't ask permission. It bruises our ego and, being forced from our sweet spot, can make us feel lost. Even though you may feel like stepping on the gas to get to and through the unknown realm in front of you, you may also feel the need to hit the brakes so you can stay in the known.

Transition is revealing. During this season our insecurities are often uncovered, and our worries exposed. Although we may "smile for the camera," the heart feels smothered by a sense of uneasiness.

Transition is inevitable. We can scream at it, cry over it, deny it, or "play possum" through it. But, the passage through change is unavoidable.

Transition is inevitable. We can scream at it, cry over it, deny it, or "play possum" through it. But, the passage is unavoidable.

SIX TRANSITION SYMPTOMS

Jacob experienced some very real symptoms that confirmed his entrance to the Season of Transition. I should note here that the same symptoms can occur during the Season of Productivity. But in that season, they usually reveal problems. In transition, those six symptoms imply change, not problems:

1. **Unsettledness**

   In his productivity, Jacob began to notice a difference in the atmosphere. His father-in-law, Laban, changed. His countenance was no longer favorable. Even though Jacob was among family, a clear sense of hostility began to grow. Jacob began to feel like a stranger, an outcast. Even though functions had not changed, their relationship began shifting. During his time of productivity, Jacob received an outpouring of appreciation and honor for the impact of his work on his in-laws. Then, in the Transition season, even though the outflow of blessing had not changed and there was no reason for disfavor, *something* happened.

Change disrupted everything. Being unsettled creates instability. Transition doesn't feel "normal!"

Unsettledness can manifest in several ways. You may start to feel some apprehension about responsibilities and communications that should be, and were, simple and smooth. Suspicion may settle around relationships and dynamics. Everything may look normal, but you still feel a little out of whack, off balance.

2. Upheaval

Jacob's unsettledness brought upheaval. And that appeared as confusion and claims of financial injustice. That shook all the tangible security and comfort that Jacob had acquired. Disputes erupted over family heirlooms; sinister plans unfolded. Jacob's long-term strategy for land and livestock fell into disarray. Jacob's life became tumultuous. Pandemonium reigned.

Upheaval disturbs the routines of life as all the planning and organization unravel. During the Season of Productivity, disorder can be logical outcomes to a problem. But, during Transition, disruption is not rational. There is no solace in disorientation.

3. Fear

After Jacob fled, Laban caught up with him and demanded an explanation. Jacob told him that he was afraid- afraid he would lose his wives, his children, and his possessions. After finding resolution of that fear, Jacob faced a new fear: He learned that Esau was coming. Jacob had to face his twin brother, the one who hated him and threatened to kill him.

The Season of Transition brings unsubstantiated fear. And, it can be erratic in what and whom it targets. You can wake up in the middle of the night, terrorized by nightmares of what the future holds. You can break out in a cold sweat thinking everything you've done is useless. Fear paralyzes our senses; it knocks our judgment askew. And that destabilizes our ability to cope with life. Fear is a horrific toxin — it can anesthetize our ability to process things appropriately, and it can make even the smallest of decisions feel mountainous. Fear is like being buried alive!

Fear paralyzes our senses; it knocks our judgment askew. And that destabilizes our ability to cope with life.

4. Distress

Along with the fear that engulfed his heart, Jacob's soul became distressed. Mental and physical oppression overwhelmed him.

During my time of Transition, my routine (and normally enjoyable) responsibilities began to strain my capacities. I stressed out over non-critical issues, and my work became too rigid. I started to view my role as a burden more than a privilege.

Distress is a painful tension that severely presses our mental and physical wellness. When you feel threatened, attacked, or pressured, your nervous system responds by releasing adrenaline and cortisol into your blood system. And cortisol increases blood sugar and suppresses the immune system. In fact, WebMD gives the critical dimensions of stress: [15]

- *43% of all adults suffer the adverse health effects of stress.*

- *75% — 90% of all doctor's office visits are for stress-related ailments and complaints.*
- *Stress can play a part in headaches, high blood pressure, heart problems, diabetes, skin conditions, asthma, arthritis, depression, and anxiety.*
- *Stress costs American industry more than $300 billion annually.*
- *The lifetime prevalence of an emotional disorder is more than 50%, often because of chronic and untreated stress.*

Distress, if left unattended, can disable your ability to function. It distorts normalcy and clouds your discernment of progress.

5. Uncertainty

When Jacob had to face his twin brother, he became uncertain. Distress cluttered his ability to think clearly — he didn't know what he should do. Should he face him? Run? Fight? Surrender? Jacob was divided in his thoughts.

Uncertainty renders us unable to act. Our mind becomes inundated with unanswerable questions that, during normal times, would have been answered quickly and surely. And hesitancy can obscure clarity of direction.

Uncertainty renders us unable to act. Our mind becomes inundated with unanswerable questions that, during normal times, would have been answered quickly and surely.

When we're caught in the transitional season, we can lose our bearings. I did; my internal navigation system felt sluggish, and I began to lose clarity of vision. Sometimes that causes a person to react to disorientation by doing things faster. I learned that doesn't make things clearer; it just gets you there quicker!

6. Relational Rupture

Jacob's transition dilemma imposed a heavy strain on his relationship with his relatives. That strain led to Jacob becoming angry with Laban; in the heat of the moment, he spoke harshly to him. Accusations abounded and the familial bond became strained. The "in-laws" felt more like "outlaws!"

A relational rupture too often brings anger, accusation, offense, snubbing, and rebuffing. And, that usually disconnects and alienates relationships.

As "justified" as a person might feel in a relational breach, nothing removes the joy from family reunions, church gatherings, neighborhood dynamics, or other relational meetings like conflict and disharmony. A Season of Transition can place severe strains on our relationships. The strength of friendship gets tested, not in good times, but in the turbulence of change.

THE FIVE LOSSES OF TRANSITION

Times of Productivity bring great increase, but Transition can weaken or remove five attributes gained and enjoyed during the Season of Productivity. Regardless of what you gained in that season, you will probably lose them, at least for a while. Buckle your seatbelt.

The Loss of Identity

We all know that Productivity can become our identity; we are known by what we do to bring money into the house. That's why personal introductions always seem to include the question, "What do you do for a living?"

But, in transitional times, that source of identity just stops. And, that can throw us into a whirlwind of bewilderment. Consider Jacob's loss of vocational uniqueness. Not only did he engage a massive relocation, but God even changed his name, from "Jacob" to "Israel." Talk about a loss of identity. Everyone knew "Jacob" for what he had done in the past, but "Israel" only reflected who he would be. As promising as his future appeared, he nevertheless lost so much of who he was. Trust me: That is painful.

For 28 years, I was known as "Mr. CCLI." The Administrators of Gospel Music (AGM) called me the "Paradigm Pioneer of Church Music." I was considered an icon in the Christian music industry. It was only natural for me to believe that was who "I" was. Transitioning out of my role brought a ghastly sense of loss.

Why do we feel such cyclonic confusion? Because the joy of our productivity persuades us that our identity is our calling. We equate "what I *do*" with "who I *am*."

Simply put, our Productivity is not our purpose. Our real identity is not what we do, but who we are. And, you find who you are in Christ, not in your performance. The Season of Transition is a precious occasion where sand castles of identity get swept away by the rising tide of God's purpose. That's why the Season of Transition is, in fact, a reset and recalibration of your true identity.

The Season of Transition is a precious occasion where sand castles of identity get swept away by the rising tide of God's purpose.

The Loss of Power

Oh, the sweet, sweet savor of "control." There is nothing like the rush of being in charge. It inflates your ego! During your time of great Productivity, you exercised authority in your realm of responsibility. The very process of making decisions revealed you had authority over people and things. Having power proves the quality of your character more than having problems. Control is intoxicating and addicting; it is a leadership "endorphin" that gets released through having power.

And then things change.

Transition deports you from the throne of your sweet spot. When your comfort throne no longer exists, you can feel completely incompetent. Why does that loss of power feel so drastic? Because our accomplishments became too important and probably inflated. Our success can make us think *we* are the source of our own ingenuity. You know; without *me*, success just won't happen. As a result, when we get removed from our strength, a sense or fear of impotence sneaks into our domain. In that moment, it is so important to stand upon the conviction that you did not create yourself. You are not the source of your potency! That's why the Season of Transition is a great gift for realigning our outlook to the truth that God is your Strength! He is your Fortress and the source of your Power!

Your ability to survive the loss of power is dependent upon your understanding and acknowledgment that the "power" was never yours!

Surviving the loss of power will bring you to a deep understanding—and confession—that the power was never yours! God gave you the power in the exact proportion needed for, and during, your Productivity.

The Loss of Input

In times of Productivity, your experience, education, and skill enable you to give perspective and wisdom that can be of great benefit to others. Your expertise is recognized and received. Of course, it feels good that people want to hear your insights. There is a wonderful sense of fulfillment in being a source of input.

And then things change.

Transition will usually take you to a place where your once-valued and welcomed input is no longer sought. When that happens, "your" wisdom finds no avenue for expression; you feel like you've become invisible. Although you could still contribute, you are no longer invited to the table for counsel. Your perspective may now even be viewed as obsolete or threatening.

> Be patient. And wait. God knows your name, your address, and your phone number. He knows where you are...

I've experienced that loss twice. The first time was when I transitioned out of my role as music pastor of our church. Even though I had conducted a large choir and orchestra, directed musical productions, and taught worship, transition meant my input was no longer welcomed. Ouch!

The second time was when I transitioned out of my role at CCLI. When all that changed, my voice was no longer invited to the table. Double ouch! In my pain, I attributed that loss to my successor; how could he cut me out of the very ministry I birthed? Then, God spoke to me clearly, "Howard, your successor is not doing this. I am! Embrace My future for you!"

That word allowed me to migrate to a place of peace. Mostly.

Understand that the pain of this loss does not come from any person; it comes from the season.

How does one adjust to no longer having a voice? It takes patience. According to Proverbs 25:11, "A word fitly spoken is like apples of gold in settings of silver." (NKJV) The phrase "fitly spoken" means "in its proper season." When your wisdom speaks in its proper season, it carries great benefit and blessing to others. If wisdom is not in alignment with its season, it cannot and will not be received. Season of Productivity wisdom may not be appropriate during the Season of Transition. So, what can you do? Be patient. And wait. God knows your name, your address, and your phone number. He knows where you are and, when it is time, He will match your input with the right season.

The Loss of Influence

You were once successful, respected, and admired. You made a difference in the lives of others. You walked in great influence and had a great impact on many people.

And then things changed.

The Season of Transition will insinuate that you are no longer respected or admired and that you will no longer make a difference in the lives of others. These veiled implications are daggers of deceit! Don't believe it!

One of the hardest moments in my Transition occurred during the Dove Awards in 2017. The previous year, I was "the voice" of CCLI, and I participated in presenting the Worship Song of the Year. I was introduced as CCLI founder and Hall of Fame Inductee. Lights! Camera! Action! But, in 2017, my successor fulfilled the CCLI presentation for the Dove Awards. Of course, that role was his proper place. But, the enemy used that incident to throw one of his deceitful daggers at me — "*your influence is over!*"

How does one endure the loss of influence? By recognizing the difference between "influence" and "prominence." Influence belongs to God; He releases it as He pleases. But prominence is just visibility. The success of productivity makes it easy to assume that your effect *on* others is because you are noticed *by* others!

Transition strips the illusions and pride away from the great achievements of Productivity. And the only path forward falls right through James 4:10, "*Humble yourselves in the sight of the Lord, and He will lift you up.*" (NKJV) Humility will help us to see that influence will always outlast prominence.

The Loss of Value

Here's a problem; the Productivity that generated success also delivers an illusion; we think our value is directly connected to the recognition and appreciation we received for our accomplishments. Equating value with Productivity distorts so much in life. Maybe that's because success typically gets measured in tangible amounts. What did you pay for your car? How much is your house worth? What is the value of your investment portfolio? How large is your estate? These answers are typically based upon "comparables" — the comparing of one thing to another.

But, comparing yourself in Transition to the way you were during your Season of Productivity can torment you with false conclusions. Have you noticed that comparison always seems to end up in the assurance you are no longer valued, that you are useless? A godly man, caught in the grip of Transition, told a friend of mine that his most painful moment was when he concluded he was worth more dead than alive. Think of how many people that deception has carried into suicide. This stuff is not a game.

If "*beauty is in the eye of the beholder,*" ask yourself, "Who is my "beholder?" Being your own beholder is perverse. But, if God is your beholder, He sees you as complete and precious. After all, He made you in His image, and there's no higher value than that.

The Season of Transition confirms His perfect plan for you. That is the path by which He moves you more clearly into your eternal purpose. The Apostle Paul described it this way — "*But we all, with unveiled face, beholding as in a mirror the glory of the Lord, are being* transformed *into the same image from glory to glory, just as by the Spirit of the Lord.*" (2 Corinthians 3:18 NASB) God decrees change *in* you so that He can move you into His completeness *for* you! For God to get you to where you are going, He has to take you from where you are! And that requires change.

In order for God to get you to where you are going, He has to take you from where you are! And that requires change.

While wrestling with an angel, Jacob dislocated his hip. And, he never walked the same way again. I assure you, Transition will change the way you walk in the future.

In 1987, our church, Bible Temple in Portland, had grown CCLI's prototype StarPraise Ministries to over 1,000 churches, all under my direction as music pastor. In late summer, Pastor Dick Iverson saw that I was leading two visions—one, the music ministry of our church, and two, StarPraise Ministries. He realized and told me I could not do both. I had to choose one.

I told Pastor Iverson that I would think and pray about it over the next two weeks, during our vacation. I loved being music pastor of our church—80-voice choir, 30-piece orchestra, worship leading, conference speaking, etc. So, I felt good about staying as the music pastor, letting someone else do all this "church copyright stuff." So, I told Pastor Iverson of my decision to stay as music pastor, and prepared for another glorious season of music ministry.

But, the very next Sunday, my heart was dead! I had no inspiration. No creativity. The preparation was burdensome. Everything felt empty. Nothing.

So, when I returned to God for a second opinion, I heard Him ask me three questions:

"Do you know My Call?"

"Yes," I replied, "I know Your Hand is on me for ministry."

"Do you know My Voice?"

"Yes, I feel confident I know when You speak to me."

"Do you know My Path?"

Uh, hmm; I was gobsmacked! I had assumed His path for me was to serve as music pastor. But He had a new path. I then knew that my ministry *for* the church was not to be confused with my ministry *in* the church.

So, when I told Pastor Iverson of my decision to discontinue being music pastor, my Season of Transition began. It was hard. The five losses of Transition hurt. But, if I had dug in my heels and resisted God, where would I now be?

The gold medal is never given to the fastest 90-meter runner for a 100-meter race!

It's hard to let go of your Season of Productivity. But, remember, you don't reach your destination of Disneyland by settling in Denver. It doesn't matter how far you've come in your life journey; you haven't finished yet. They don't give the gold medal to the fastest 90-meter runner for a 100-meter race! You need to go the full distance in order to reach your destination.

Your life path is probably not a simple and straight road. It is more likely you will travel a series of convoluted roadways. But, if you follow God, He will lead you throughout your entire life journey. And when you look back, you see that the path was seamlessly predestined. Looking back is like looking at a tapestry from the top! After gazing so long at the underside's apparent chaos, moving to the top-side view will help us see the awesome beauty and perfection of His plans.

Yes, it is hard and painful to let go of a Season of Productivity. The Season of Transition has an undeniable impact on our emotional, mental, physical, and spiritual wellness. However, this season necessitates the practicing of this important truth — How we handle where we are coming from will determine how we flourish in where we are going.

Columnist Ellen Goodman once wrote, "There is a trick to the graceful exit. It begins with a vision to recognize that a job, a life stage, a relationship is over— and to let it go. It means leaving what is over without denying its validity or its past importance in our lives. It involves a sense of future, a belief that every exit line is also an entry, that we are moving up rather than out."[16]

If you look to your tomorrow with the eyes of yesterday, you cannot see the beauty of where He is leading you, and how He is perfecting you. And, you cannot progress to your future unless you let go of your past.

FAMILY

My parents, Ernie & Ida; my sister, Myrna; my brother, Rod, and me

Our wedding day – February 10, 1973 with both sets of parents

The Kirkpatrick Clan 2014 (4 generations)

The Rachinski Clan 2018 (4 generations)

Dyane (center), Deryk (left), Dryden (right)

Our family in Maui

My sister, Myrna, and my
"bro-in-law" Ron. Our battle against
her cancer ultimately helped me see
the beautiful mystery of life seasons.

3 days after Rod was diagnosed
with brain cancer

Mom, Dad & I say
goodbye to Rod

MUSIC & CCLI

Early music ministry with the New Dimensions – 1976 Pacific National Exhibition

New Dimensions Reunion Concert, 2010

Early Worship Ministry with my father-in-law, 1977 – Taiwan

May, 1985 – launched Starpraise Ministries, the prototype for CCLI

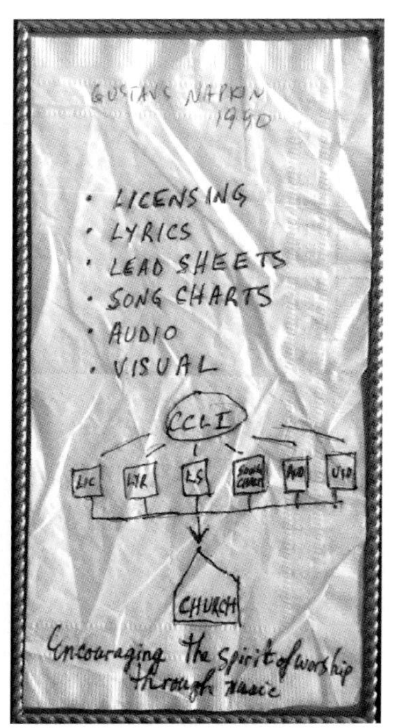

1990 – "Gustav's Napkin", while at a restaurant, I quickly wrote what God said we were to do

CCLI officially launched October 1988, now serving 250,000+ churches

1995 – North America office

2008 – CCLI North America staff, our 20th Anniversary

All photos courtesy of CCLI

2013 – CCLI North America Admin Team

2015 – CCLI Global Team

Geoff Booker – MD, CCLI Europe, 1992 – 2005

Table Mountain, Cape Town, with Malcolm Hawker, my CCLI Successor

Our very dear friends – Victor & Kathy Anfuso

One of my favorite moments – my mentor, Victor Anfuso, praying for me (CCLI)

2014 – CCLI Global Executive Team (Andy Bodkin, Gary Christensen, George Ross, Rod, Malcolm)

Terry & Shari Iverson were with me right from start of CCLI in 1988

My spiritual father – Pastor Dick Iverson – who encouraged the formation of CCLI while I was the Worship Pastor at Bible Temple in Portland

Since 1988, I have had the privilege of having these amazing men as my Pastor – Dick Iverson, Frank Damazio & Marc Estes

David Garratt presenting me with engraving of my favorite song – "Highest Place"

Being interviewed in Seoul, Korea on the launch of our CCLI Korea office

WITH ANDRAÉ & SANDRA CROUCH

1974 – at Andraé's house in Woodland Hills, CA

On one of our many trips to Maui

2007 – Celebrating Andraé's 40th year in ministry

2008 at CCLI's 20th Anniversary Banquet

With Sandra & Donna

2016 HALL OF FAME INDUCTION

Eddie DeGarmo was my inductor

Ed Cash led a worship medley for the ceremony

All photos courtesy of Gospel Music Association

INDUSTRY FRIENDS

David Crowder

Bart Millard – "I Can Only Imagine"

Sherman Andrus

Chris Tomlin

Michael W. Smith

Darlene Zschech

All photos courtesy of CCLI

Israel Houghton

Donnie McClurkin

Jackie Patillo, President, GMA
& Demetrius Alexander

Point of Grace, with Rod
& Gary Christensen

Dr. Jack Hayford (CCLI)

David Garratt – Founder,
Scripture in Song (CCLI)

Matt Redman

Steven Curtis Chapman

Lincoln Brewster

Beth Moore

Pat Boone & Debby Boone-Ferrer

Mark Lowry

Russ Taff

Bill & Gloria Gaither, and my daughter, Dyane

Morris Chapman

Tramaine Hawkins

2016 – Special award from Church Music Publishers Association, Mike Harland, President

Geoff Lorenz and the famous "Lorinki Cup"

2016 – With Kari Jobe as we present the Dove Award Worship Song of the Year (GMA)

Taya Smith & JD Douglass – Hillsong United

With Amy Grant and Michael W. Smith

Tamela Mann, Dr. Bobby Jones, Eddie DeGarmo

Jim Van Hook (CCLI)

Bishop Timothy Dudley Smith, Hymnwriter

Chris Tomlin

Darlene Zschech (CCLI)

Michael W. Smith and Sandra Crouch

Governor Mike Huckabee

Danny Gokey - American Idol

Steve Scheidler, Ken Malmin & Tim Nashif at
St. Andrews and Pebble Beach Golf Courses.
Dear friends who have walked many
fairways in many seasons together.

As Donna and I enter a new season of God's perpetual life

CHAPTER EIGHT

THE SEASON OF REFRESHING

Scripture Reference: Genesis 45:26, 27

OK, it's time for a break!

Chapter 6 examined how the Season of Famine cleans out our spiritual system (I'm sure you remember the "souloscopy"), builds our endurance, reveals the quality of our sincerity, and prepares us for future enrichment. And, Chapter 7 tore you from your delightful Season of Productivity and pulled you through the pain of Transition. Both chapters also revealed why each season is such a gift. Famine and Transition bring deep change and renewal. In fact, no other season does what those painful periods do.

But, the grueling processes at work in both chapters can be exhausting. They leave us in profound need of the cool breezes of refreshment. That is what this chapter is about!

In Jacob's Season of Famine, the melodic song of purpose that had once sounded loud and clear probably became a distant and muffled refrain. His family had followed his direction, trusted his counsel, and depended on his wisdom. And, for what? The beautiful story ended when Joseph was reportedly killed by a wild beast. Not only was Jacob's heart broken, but his heritage was surely dead. His great "promise" did not seem transferable to anyone. He was finished.

All the emptiness, loneliness, and dejection of his long Season of Famine was over, overwhelmed in Jacob's new Season of Refreshing.

But then, something unimaginable happened. Jacob received astounding news, "Joseph is alive!" What? Could his son and his great heritage have possibly survived?

That pronouncement was so unbelievable that it overflowed Jacob's capacity to receive it—he passed out! The marvelous news was exhilarating, stunning, too good to be true! Losing Joseph had been so severe. Jacob must have had many hopes and dreams over the years for some kind of miracle. Perhaps those hopes had died, or maybe Jacob just learned to live with the perpetual pain of loss. But, then the pain stopped. Jacob was revived!

His dreams, hopes, promises, and his life purpose all experienced a rebirth; Jacob was immersed in the river of restoration. All the emptiness, loneliness, and dejection of his long Season of Famine ended, overwhelmed by the new Season of Refreshing.

The Merriam-Webster Dictionary defines "revive" as "*to return to consciousness or life; to restore from a depressed, inactive, or unused state; to bring back; to renew in the mind or memory.*"[17] Revival always comes after the seasons that bring us to depletion, exhaustion, and injury. Any word beginning with "re" always means "again" or "anew." That's why the pain of despair, famine, and transition come first. *Re*vival follows. God uses the painful seasons to build character into His people. In His own time, that character development will prepare and position us for renewal. The anguish of suffocation greatly increases our appreciation for fresh air.

WHAT IS THE SEASON OF REFRESHING?

The Season of Refreshing carries abundant infusions of His renewal into our spirit, reawakening and reinvigorating us for the next phase of our life purpose. "Season" might be too generous a description for this occurrence, as Refreshing can become realized as both short bursts of breathability and longer durations of bliss. Those moments, when embraced, will revitalize our existence.

> The Refreshing comes at an appointed time. It visits "in its season" – it has a start and it has a stop.

Several years ago, when we lived in Bellingham, WA, near beautiful Lake Whatcom, Donna's uncle had a Hobie Cat (a small sailing catamaran), which he stored at my father-in-law's house. Dad Kirkpatrick took me out on my "maiden voyage" and showed me how to handle the mainsail and the lines. No problem! I felt like I understood all the intricacies of captaining this vessel! The next day, I took my brother, Rod, out for his maiden voyage.

"You know how to handle this thing?" he asked.

"Sure," I confidently replied—I didn't see any merit to admitting that this would be my virgin voyage alone at the helm. As we slowly drifted away from shore in an almost windless condition, we bobbed along in eerie stillness. I started to think of the excuses for why we weren't sailing. Rod was polite even though we were dead in the water. Finally, we felt the wind pick up; I quickly barked out helmsman orders to my brother in anticipation for the moment. I tightened the lines, trimmed the mainsail and jib, and positioned the Hobie Cat in readiness for a beam wind. And a beam wind we got! When the fierce wind caught our sails, we exploded across the lake like we were shot out of a cannon. I was elated as the Hobie Cat rose up on one pontoon.

Rod seemed thrilled with my mastery until he noticed our rapid and precarious approach to the opposite shoreline. "Prepare to tack," I shouted as I released the boom line and thrust the rudder 90 degrees. The boom line zinged… and right at that moment, I remembered my father-in-law's instruction about tacking, "Make sure you duck!" I almost made it. The boom clipped the back of my head just enough to knock me spread-eagled across the trampoline. Rod's screams—"Howard! Howard! Howard!"—brought me back to consciousness. We quickly and carefully returned to safety.

Aside from near decapitation, that moment of taking full advantage of the wind gave me the best description for the Season of Refreshing—EXHILARATION. The Season of Refreshing floods a person with excitement and elation that purges weariness and exhaustion. In that moment, nothing else mattered. There wasn't any circumstance, experience, or emptiness that could overshadow the complete infusion of delight that comes during the Season of Refreshing.

My Refreshing sometimes came like a cool mist on my face after a scorching day. At other times, it felt like a savory meal after a period of starvation. By any description, the Refreshing season is exquisite! I was replenished with all that had been depleted in my seasons of despair and famine.

I've also come to see that Refreshing rarely comes in one period of time. It is, I think, more likely to arrive in timely moments all along our journey. It can also be intertwined, like a double helix, in and throughout all your calling seasons. In church history, extended seasons of Refreshing have often been identified as spiritual "movements," bringing an awakening or revival among specific communities of believers.

In Deuteronomy 11:14, Moses told the Israelites that the Lord would give them "rain for your land in its season..." (NKJV) The Refreshing comes at an appointed time. It visits "in its season;" it starts and it stops.

REPENTANCE: THE PRECURSOR TO REFRESHING

Did you know that you must prepare your heart for a Season of Refreshing?

That is true even if you do not see the cloud of refreshing rain on the horizon. Even if you think everything is collapsing around you, you must prepare. How can you prepare for Refreshing when you don't see it coming? We all carry an extraordinary treasure, our will! By that God-given part of our composition, we can still govern in calamity. As my dear friend, Pastor Glen Roachelle, says, "When you can't control your environment, you can still rule your spirit!" Regardless of your life circumstance, you can still position your heart to receive revival.

Of course, you can also disqualify your heart from experiencing the Refreshing. If you allow circumstances to wound you, harden your heart, make you angry at God, and live in bitterness over God's perceived injustices, you could miss the great Refreshing that is surely moving toward you. Some have become confused by the apparent breakdown between God's promise and God's performance. That and other failures to comprehend His ways can disqualify some from receiving His great mercy and kindness. Sometimes, failure enters the heart through deception. You cannot understand why God didn't do what you hoped, prayed for, or thought He promised. You start thinking, "God, you betrayed me; You let me down!" You may become wounded by an incident and blame God for such an injustice or disappointment. Through anger at God's "failure," you may feel your trust in Him begin to evaporate. Such experiences and perceptions can allow bitterness to fill your heart as you try to justify your actions. Sadly, that can become a tragic path that jeopardizes renewal.

> The first step in preparing your heart for a Season of Refreshing is to abolish the thought path of the past and reset your mind to the hope of the future.

Remember, no matter what you face, "Guard your heart above all else, for it determines the course of your life." (Proverbs 4:23 (NLT) Be quick to hear Peter's admonition in Acts 3:19 (NKJV), "Repent therefore and be converted, that your sins may be blotted out, so *that times of refreshing may come* from the presence of the Lord." (italics mine)[18]

When we think of the word "repent," we usually think of admitting sin and thereby alleviating guilt. While that contains some truth, it falls so short of the power contained in this word. Let's look at some specifics of how repentance prepares our heart for the Season of Refreshing.

1. Repentance <u>clears out old thought patterns.</u>

The Greek word for "repent" is "*metanoeō*," which means "to think differently, reconsider."[19] Naturally, our thoughts get shaped by past experiences, both good and bad. But that also means our past can harden into thought patterns about the future. Our outlook for tomorrow can be altered by the events of yesterday.

We tend to aim at where we are going by where we have been. Therefore, the first step in preparing your heart for His Season of Refreshing is to hit the reset in your mind. Turn from the past to the hope of the future. Be renovated in your thinking.

2. Repentance changes the old habit patterns.

The Greek word for "be converted" is "*epistrephō*," which means "to revert, turn about."[20] We are all creatures of habit. Habits are not bad; bad habits are bad!

For example, as hard as it may be for readers to believe, I've been told that my otherwise wonderful attributes are sometimes not evident on the golf course. I. Love. Golf! I am not great at golf, I just love golf. I am also a perfectionist and, sometimes, my personality and my golf passion are at cross-purposes with each other! A few years ago, I began to allow my displeasure to send my golf club soaring through the heavens like a whirling helicopter blade. Over time, that became a habit, a bad one.

> "Every morning, I deliberately choose not to be offended by anyone." – *Michael W. Smith*

One time, I was playing golf in Nashville with my good friend Stan Moser. On one hole, I had a very easy approach to the green, and I shanked it wide right and very short. After observing my whirling helicopter blade display, Stan said, "Howard, remember, one billion people in China don't even know you play this game." Ouch! His words exposed a bad habit and convicted me. That's when I began repenting, converting to new behavior.

The Message seems to speak directly to me with its interpretation of Ephesians 4:22-24 (MSG): "Since, then, we do not have the excuse of ignorance, everything—and I do mean everything—connected with that old way of life has to go. It's rotten through and through. Get rid of it! And then take on an entirely new way of life—a God-fashioned life, a life renewed from the inside and working itself into your conduct as God accurately reproduces His character in you."

3. Repentance leads us to forgive those who have offended us.

Let's face it, our hearts are vulnerable to being wounded by others. It happens; you can't prevent offenses from occurring. But, you can stop the subsequent infection from permeating and killing your life purpose or your joy.

During the ordeal of my brother's struggle against brain cancer, I was hurt deeply by some family members. People never know how a great life-and-death battle will affect them. I'm sure everyone was coping with Rod's condition the best way they could. But, the pain of that relational breach pulled me into the scorching flames of offense. But, through the kindness of God, I saw that I had a choice—I could let the offense fester in my soul and destroy my health, or I could forgive them. I chose to forgive. Every day, I had to deliberately declare, "*Lord, I forgive* __________." The process of forgiveness began with the confession of my mind, and then radiated out to my heart.

My first real contact with Michael W. Smith was when CCLI sponsored his first "Evening of Worship" at the GMA Conference in 2001. The reception we received from the gospel music industry to this worship service was overwhelming! As the service ended, Michael walked off the stage, hugged me, and lifted me right off my feet! Years later, Michael came to our office, just to say thank you to the staff for all the work they were doing to help churches. In that meeting, I asked him what one key had helped guide him through his career. He said, "Every morning, I deliberately choose not to become offended by anyone."

Relational conflicts do not justify grudges or allow offenses. Those who carry them should pause and take a deep whiff of this scriptural smelling salt: "If you, God, kept records on wrong-doings, who would stand a chance? As it turns out, forgiveness is your habit, and that's why you're worshiped." (Psalms 130:3-4 MSG)

THE PURPOSE OF REFRESHING

Refreshing turns dry deserts into fertile fields. When my time of Refreshing arrived, it was just splendidly delicious! It revitalized me for my future.

As I mentioned previously, my brother Rod and I were "joined at the heart." But, it wasn't always that way. We were six years apart in age and that can be a big span for kids. In time, that span widened into a chasm of estrangement. To me, in those years, Rod was an annoying little pest, and I had no desire to hang out with him. And, Rod resented me because he felt Dad spent more time playing with me. Although I wanted nothing to do with my little brother, I also wouldn't let anyone hurt him.

One day, as Rod was being taunted by a couple of bullies, I unexpectedly walked into the altercation. Surprising anger surged through my veins—no one was going to mess with my 11-year-old brother! I grabbed one of the bullies by the scruff of his neck, lifted him up and plopped him down onto the top of a 4-foot high tree stump (sadly, the other kid vanished in terror). With every "voice of God" inflection I could muster, I said, "Don't. You. Move," and "Don't you ever mess with my brother again! Do you understand me?" He shuddered his agreement. I turned away, put my arm around my little brother, and triumphantly walked him home. A few minutes down the road, Rod said to me, "Wow! I didn't even think you liked me!"

I assume the bully eventually found a way to get down from that stump.

But, Rod and I still remained distanced from each other for several more years. Then, in 1974, something happened. Our church experienced a special wave of revival. After one powerful time of worship, our church participated in a different expression of communion. We were each given a chunk of bread and then instructed to share the bread and pray with others. Immediately, I felt the need to do this with Rod. But, he felt very reluctant to "break bread" with me.

Rod didn't see me approach him. When I tapped him on the shoulder, he turned around, our eyes locked, and we melted into each other's arms. In that moment, our hearts became fused together. Our relationship became right in the rains of refreshing. The Season of Refreshing both deepened my intimacy with God and healed my relationships with others. I became keenly aware that He was NEAR! It was "first love" all over again and your heart feels whole and full!

Refreshing revealed and nourished new heart resources for my future life-purpose. I no longer felt incapable. I had renewed energy from God to do what I still needed to do. Refreshing recalibrated my vision so that I could see my "go-forward" with more assurance. The seasons of Transition, Despair, and Famine had made me feel confused and uncertain about my purpose and future. I could now see my purpose more clearly.

Central Oregon is "high desert" and, consequently, drier than western Oregon. In the summer of 2018, many forest fires surrounded us, the heavy smoke obscuring our view of the Cascade Mountains. For several weeks, the air quality was dangerous, and our ability to see remained shrouded. Then, one evening a shower rolled in. The next morning, the brilliant clarity of the Cascade Mountains stood in beautiful and vivid contrast to the clarion blue sky. It felt good to breathe fresh air again.

Seasons of Refreshing often remove the smoke of our despair and famine and surround us with beautiful clarity.

My time of Refreshing also realigned me to His purpose in my life walk. The smoke and dryness, although fulfilling His purpose for that season, had clouded what He had called me to do.

On a hypothetical journey to the sun, just one degree of deviation means you would miss the sun by 1.6 million miles! Refreshing gets you exactly back on course so that you don't miss the mark!

How marvelous that God brings Famine and aridity for the work that only they can do. But, then in the fullness of His time, He also brings the rain and cool breezes of Refreshing that drive the smoke away. By restoring clarity, He also course-corrects and recalibrates our journey so we can see the target of His intention.

Refreshing will refill your faith-tank. The rigors of life can deplete your spirit and, in that sense of emptiness, fear can taunt your mind. At times, I even felt a sense of panic. Looking back, I understand it; I had been shaken by loss and by the helplessness to do anything about it. But then, the Season of Refreshing reconnected me to my awareness of His unfailing love. "I will fear NO evil!"

The Season of Refreshing fortified my courage. My confidence that "all things are possible" returned. It also recalibrated my vision so that I could see my "go-forward" with more assurance. Various circumstances had made me feel confused and uncertain about my purpose and future. An accumulation of incidents had developed cataracts on my soul — I had lost the ability to see my journey clearly. But, Refreshing was a moment where God performed "laser-surgery" on the eyes of my heart, and I could once again see my purpose in life.

Finally, the Season of Refreshing healed my spirit from the wounds of criticism and failure. Sometime later, I learned about "Lingchi," an ancient form of torture (until it became illegal in 1905) in China. It killed people through "a thousand cuts." This torture brought a slow death through slicing the body multiple times and removing small pieces of flesh. So, although a person could survive the loss of blood from a few cuts, the continual succession of cuts would ultimately cause a person to bleed out.

Our journey takes us through many "dangers, toils, and snares," all of which inflict small slices to our soul. Those losses, missteps, defeats, deficiencies, weaknesses, and failures all deliver small cuts to our life purpose. And, for some of us, some cuts are self-inflicted! We should always refuse to speak the Accuser's assaults against ourselves. Calling yourself "stupid" and voicing other accusations all play a role in your "Soul Lingchi." Refreshing is like a healing ointment. It cleanses and heals your soul from the cuts that have accrued throughout all the seasons. My life found healing and refreshment — I could, at last, breathe again!

The Refreshing season also allowed me to see the difference between surrender and resignation. Surrender is when you leave the fight; resignation is when the fight leaves you. That helped me see I could leave the fighting up to Him, and *that* helped to put the fight back in me. Through all that, my confidence was restored, my soul was replenished, and I found the strength to continue.

"ABRAHAM STAGGERED NOT AT THE PROMISE OF GOD."

One week before Thanksgiving 2016, Donna came into our bedroom bowed over in intense pain. Her misery finally subsided enough to get through the weekend, but the following Monday a specialist examined her and ran some tests. Early Tuesday morning, her primary care doctor called and told her to get into the ER immediately—her liver enzymes were 10 times higher than they should be. I quickly drove her to the nearest hospital. Upon arrival, I texted my friend, Glen Roachelle, to let him know what was going on. After a quick prayer, Glen texted me back: "As I prayed, I saw Donna sitting in a boat that was being rowed by Jesus. Tell her to sit back and relax, because Jesus has His hands on the oars." Donna immediately "inhaled" that word into her spirit and settled into His peace.

The doctors were concerned Donna might have some blockage in her bile duct, so after a CT Scan, they inserted stents into her bile duct via an endoscopic retrograde cholangiopancreatography (ERCP). Donna had to spend Thanksgiving weekend in the hospital while I became the chief cook for our traditional family Thanksgiving dinner.

On the Tuesday after Thanksgiving, we met with the hospital's oncologist. He had bad news. Donna had a ½ centimeter tumor in her pancreas. He suggested immediate surgery, a Whipple procedure. Those who undergo a successful Whipple procedure may have a five-year survival rate of up to 25%.

Donna calmly and peacefully thanked the doctor for his information and said that we would follow up with her personal doctor to assess next steps. Where was my sweetheart getting such amazing tranquility? This was serious; her father had died from the same condition.

Her doctor referred Donna to one of the top pancreatic oncologists in our region. After the exam, we agreed she would have an endoscopic ultrasound and biopsy on Thursday, December 13. We prayed.

The day before Donna's procedure, I was doing my usual power-walking prayer time on the treadmill. I routinely finish my exercise with a little mental game; I try to make the total calories burned and the total miles walked end on even numbers. When the treadmill stopped, I ended up with 440.1 calories burned. I thought to myself, "*Hmm, I took one step more than I should have.*" At that very moment, I heard Him whisper, "Whatever you target your prayer on, I will go one step beyond."

I ran up our stairs and told Donna what had just happened. My spirit just groaned each word. That night, our lead pastor and several elders came over for a focused time of prayer. Naturally, I told them what the Lord said to me.

One elder asked, "What do you want to target your prayer on?"

"That Donna's tumor be gone!" And, that's how we prayed.

The next day, Donna went in for her procedure. My daughter-in-law and I sat in the waiting room, waiting. And waiting. The procedure was to take 45 minutes, but we waited for 50 minutes, and then 55, 60, 75 minutes. My heart was pounding as the enemy screamed lies. But my mind remained anchored in a biblical truth — "*Abraham staggered not at the promise of God!*" My spirit became resolved, "I will stand on His promise!"

Finally, the buzzer went off, and we could go see her. Minutes later, the doctor came into the room and told us, "We looked everywhere. We could see where the CT scan showed there was something, but it's not there anymore. I don't know what to say." The following month, Donna went in for a second endoscopic ultrasound, to make sure they didn't miss anything. It found nothing. Donna was healed.

The doctor again said, "I have no explanation."

Donna told him, "I do. We believe in prayer. God healed me." The doctor said, "I like that; I'll put that in the report."

And, in early 2018, Donna's sister, who underwent chemotherapy after being diagnosed with breast cancer, was pronounced "cancer free" by her doctor.

Our son, Dryden? He has persevered through his nearly two years of neurological therapy and is currently pursuing a Theology degree at Portland Bible College. His brain has healed!

THE RHYTHM OF REST

While the Season of Refreshing reinvigorates us for the next phase of our life, it can also bring new rhythms of rest. That's when I discovered that secret cadence of life. I had misunderstood the biblical idea of rest. Perhaps you have too.

We most commonly view rest as a need brought about by fatigue and weariness. Although that is a proper association for the word "rest," it is not the whole story. Genesis 2:2-3 (NKJV) tells us, "*And on the seventh day God ended His work which He had done, and He rested on the seventh day from all His work which He had done. Then God blessed the seventh day and sanctified it, because in it He rested from all His work which God had created and made.*"[21]

What? God rested? Why? Was He tired? No; God doesn't get fatigued. So, what does it mean to rest?

I came to see the rhythm of rest as taking regular breaks, stopping the work in order to see and appreciate what has already been completed. What does that mean?

First, it is a time to *reflect* on what has been accomplished. I learned to develop a routine of carefully considering life's beneficial and favorable moments. After all, God took time to recognize that creation had been finished and that it was good! Do you think that may be a pattern for us? No matter what season of life we may find ourselves in, we should take time to consider what has been accomplished instead of what was not.

It's easy for us to focus on the bad or incomplete stuff. But it is more important to identify what has been completed and *is good*...every day, in every Life Season (even those called Famine, Despair, or Transition). It is important to ponder and appreciate the positive and beautiful times.

Like most golfers, I have hit more bad shots than good ones. But, I've noticed that I don't remember my bad shots the next day. I only re-play the good. When you engage the rhythm of rest, you allow your mind to be filled with good, lovely, inspiring, and encouraging thoughts. As you consider a completed project or beautiful outcome, no matter how minuscule it may seem, you are replenishing your soul with the resolve that will enable you to go on.

Second, the rhythm of rest allows time to *savor* the good moments, to enjoy the distinctive richness of a relationship, a day, an event with great delight and pleasure. We can find the good in every season. Like so much of life, it all depends on what and how you see.

I love to barbeque steaks for our family get-togethers, and Donna has a great knack for seasoning those steaks. It would be tragic to simply devour the steak without savoring the flavor! The movie *What About Bob?* features a scene where Bob Wiley is having dinner with the Marvin family. With every bite, Bob expresses his great delight with a hearty "Mmm, mmm, mmm." Every single bite. That is a great illustration of savoring the good.

As a "results-oriented" type of personality, I have often hurried along from one accomplishment to the next project. I relished doing things quickly. Sadly, that caused me to lose the joy of stopping and enjoying the completion of something. When you delight in the value of what has been accomplished, you release the contentment, within yourself, others, and your whole environment. And, contentment is a catalyst for wellness. Yes, it is important to "stop and smell the roses," even in the midst of thorns.

Third, celebrate what has been achieved. Take time to mark and honor the triumph. Congratulate and cherish everyone who contributed to the effort. When we first started CCLI, we walked under the normal pressures of being a start-up company. Even as we faced the "tyranny of survival," we also learned to take time to celebrate our achievements. If we reached or exceeded a monthly goal, we had a pizza party to celebrate that accomplishment. If we had a bad month, we had a pizza party and celebrated each other.

In the rhythm of rest, celebrating encourages commitment. When you take the time to hold an "accomplishment festival," you are infusing your spirit with the energy for continuation. Rah-rah moments are essential in the rhythm of rest. As the Apostle Paul tells us, *"Summing it all up, friends, I'd say you'll do best by filling your minds and meditating on things that are true, noble, reputable, authentic, compelling, gracious—the best, not the worst; the beautiful, not the ugly; things to praise, not things to curse."* (Philippians 4:8 MSG)

The rhythm of rest is important in any season. It should ripple through all of life like a stream of encouragement and renewal.

A FINAL THOUGHT ON THE SEASON OF REFRESHING

Times of Refreshing are so exhilarating that we sometimes want to commemorate or perpetuate the occasion. We want to monumentalize the moment! The Apostle Peter felt that way during one of his Refreshing moments—the mount of transfiguration. He was an eyewitness to a phenomenal event, God's Glory appearing on Jesus. Amid that sensory overload moment, Peter decided it would be good to build a tabernacle, not only for Jesus, but for Moses and Elijah who also appeared during the transfiguration. God had to admonish Peter by reminding him of what the reason for the Refreshing was about—His Son! And that should also instruct us. Human zeal or excitement can align our Season of Refreshing to the wrong reason.

The Season of Refreshing is not our destiny — it is an infilling so that we can reach our destiny.

Remember this as you persevere through your trials and your adversity. And be assured God will send a Season of Refreshing, and just when you really need it. Let it bring renewal for your journey.

CHAPTER NINE

THE SEASON OF IMPARTATION

Scripture Reference: Genesis 47:7,10; Genesis 48:2,15; Genesis 49:28

Throughout his life, Jacob had known great abundance and joy. And, he also knew exhaustion, depletion, and sorrow.

And then he was old; fewer days lay ahead than he had already lived. Jacob could have spent the rest of his life pining for those past "good" seasons. He could also have lived out his remaining sunsets bemoaning past failures. It would also have been easy for Jacob to assume that he had achieved his life's purpose. But, his purpose was still incomplete. One more season awaited him, Impartation. Jacob spent the remaining 17 years of his life there.

WHAT IS THE SEASON OF IMPARTATION?

The Merriam-Webster Dictionary defines impartation as "giving, conveying, bestowing; granting a part or share of;

communicating the knowledge of."[22] Of course, in order to give, convey, and bestow something, one must first acquire, hold, and cultivate something. That was certainly true of Jacob. As a result, God adorned his life with wisdom and wealth.

Jacob's previous seasons had focused on cultivating *his* personal calling and character so that he could flourish in *his* purpose. But, even more, his life had brought and endowed him with an accumulation of assets for his final and ultimate Life Season. The Impartation season would focus Jacob on the purpose of *others*.

In the previous Life Seasons, you are a steward *of* your life purpose. In the later season of Impartation, you become a statesman *for* your life purpose.

Impartation is the time of transferring your treasures and blessings to the generations that follow. In the previous Life Seasons, you are a steward *of* your life purpose. In the later Season of Impartation, you become a statesman *for* your life purpose. And, that redirection of focus generates a significant surge of value for those in your lineage. This final season is a rewarding and purposeful time when you convey all that has been bestowed upon you to others.

THE TWO JACOB BLESSINGS

Let's summarize Jacob's story. Esau and Jacob were twins, born to Isaac and Rebekah, with Esau being the older. It was customary for the father to convey a special blessing to the firstborn son. However, Jacob's mother, Rebekah, knew that it was God's will for Jacob to be blessed. So, she arranged for Jacob to supplant his twin and receive the firstborn blessing (which was rightfully

Esau's) from their father. Rebekah's plan worked, and Jacob received, not just one, but two special blessings from his father.

THE BLESSING OF BIRTHRIGHT

Isaac first gave the "Blessing of Birthright," a blessing of Jacob's physical, emotional, mental, and spiritual dimensions. That was his heritage; it served as the framework for his life. Like Jacob, we all have received certain elements that serve as the framework for our existence.

For example, have you noticed the growing genealogical fascination in our society? It is one of today's top hobbies. It is also big business, as evidenced by the sale of *Ancestry.com* for $1.6 billion in October 2012. That is because people seek a recognizable identity in a civilization that is increasingly characterized by anonymity. We all need to know who we are and that we matter!

If you detest who you are, then you weaken who you can be.

Unfortunately, that kind of research tends to make us focus on the negative traits passed to us through our respective bloodlines. Subsequently, many people compile psychological alibis and blame-transference patterns as a justification for not taking ownership of personal behavior and actions. "*It's my father's fault I am this way. My third-grade teacher did that to me... My coach was too hard on me. Why couldn't I have been born in that family? Why wasn't I...*"

How you view your heritage impacts how you convey your legacy. If you detest who you are, then you weaken who you can be.

Before you can impart life to others, you must first accept, with gratefulness, the sanctity of the Blessing of Birthright. You must have God's view of your life.

Psalm 139:14 -16 (MSG) masterfully captures the Blessing of Birthright — "I thank you, High God — "You're breathtaking! Body and soul, I am marvelously made! I worship in adoration — what a creation! You know me inside and out, You know every bone in my body; You know exactly how I was made, bit by bit, how I was sculpted from nothing into something. Like an open book, You watched me grow from conception to birth; all the stages of my life were spread out before You, the days of my life all prepared before I'd even lived one day." You have been inextricably and wonderfully fashioned exactly as God has purposed!"

"I am not hiring you for what you *can't* do; I am hiring you for what you *can* do!"

When you really understand the Blessing of Birthright, you see that what you may view as "stubbornness" inherited from your father is really "determination." That "assertiveness" the family attributes to your mother is really "confidence." What you often see as a flaw is just a misunderstanding of a character trait that God built into you. God created you and deposited special gifts in you. He calls those gifts "good and perfect" (James 1: 17, 18). Maybe you should too!

In 2005, as I was hiring a new managing director for our CCLI Europe operations, my candidate of choice met with me for a final interview. He gave me a file containing some personality and aptitude testing that, he said, explained some of his "deficiencies." I laid the file aside, looked in his eyes, and said, "I am not hiring you for what you *can't* do; I am hiring you for what you *can* do!" He was, of course, stunned by my response.

How I viewed him instilled new confidence within him. For the next 11 years, he led CCLI Europe with great success.

You can optimize your Season of Impartation by seeing and accepting yourself (and others) just as God does!

Identify, accept, and appreciate those God-given attributes given to you. Recognize His deposit in you. As the Lord prepares you and situations, impart what He gave you with confidence.

THE BLESSING OF PROMISE

"May God Almighty bless you, and make you fruitful and multiply you, that you may be an assembly of peoples. And give you the blessing of Abraham, to you and your descendants with you, that you may inherit the land in which you are a stranger, which God gave to Abraham." Genesis 28:3-4 NKJV

In addition to the Blessing of Birthright, Jacob also received The Blessing of Promise from his father. That was a blessing of his legacy. God created him for a purpose that would impact many generations. Not only did Jacob receive a blessing on his origins, he was also given a blessing for where he was going.

> The Blessing of Promise is the wisdom and expertise God has developed *in* you, so that it can be delivered to others *from* you!

The Blessing of Promise is the wisdom and expertise God has developed *in* you so that it can be delivered to others *from* you! Your life purpose is not only (or primarily) intended for your personal fulfillment; it is given to reproduce an abundant yield in the lives of others.

No matter how successful you have been in life, you will never achieve the ultimate purpose of fulfillment if it's only about you. No amount of personal accomplishment or abundance can satisfy your life's purpose without engaging the Blessing of Promise for those who follow.

The Lord has given me a passion for caring for others and helping them achieve their potential. But, as satisfying as it is for me to function in my passion, it pales compared to seeing my children (and grandchildren) caring for others. I have a passion for worshiping God. I love His Presence! However, that comes nowhere near the joy of seeing my children and grandchildren passionately worshiping God. That completes me!

At a church conference in 2008, a young lady told me, "You may not remember me, but in 1985, you came to our church in Calgary. And, after one of your teaching sessions, you told me that the Lord would deposit in me a seed of worship, and that I would impact others with that seed. I just want you to know that your word came true, and I am now the worship pastor of my church and am teaching others how to worship God. I just want to say thank you for your word." That kind of report made (and still makes) my life worthwhile!

Impartation is optimized by giving to others what God has given to you. The Blessing of Birthright brings success in life and the Blessing of Promise enables our legacy. Your discovery of the blessings of Birthright and Promise will enlighten you, and your deployment of them will enrich you.

WHAT IS THE PURPOSE FOR THE SEASON OF IMPARTATION?

The first time I held my first baby in my arms, waterfalls cascaded down my face. I was an emotional blob as I looked into that bundle of our seed, our replication (a breathtaking moment repeated with the birth of my other two babies). That precious, innocent, created, flesh-of-my-flesh gem had just transformed me from a man into a father!

And, in that beautiful metamorphosis of my identity, I began to understand the majesty of Impartation—my children were not born for my personal fulfillment; I was responsible to love and cultivate them in the Lord.

We all live to impart value and make a positive investment in the lives of others. That investment targets two arenas, tangible and intangible, in which we convey the blessings of our life.

THE TANGIBLE

When Jacob was an old man and an alien in Egypt, he continued to worship the God of his grandfather Abraham and his father Isaac. Although the Egyptians had their own complex polytheistic religion, Jacob did not despise or reject them. Instead of settling into retirement or reaction, he simply and naturally conveyed the blessings and enrichment from his blessed life to his surrounding culture.

> I see a tangible arena as any practical issue in society that needs help.

Those who know and serve the Lord walk in the call and joy of serving others in society. Very often, that service takes us into practical arenas where people desperately need help. That very tangible arena could be found in the ravages of poverty where people lack food, clothing, or shelter, or perhaps within the devastation from floods, tornados, fires, or earthquakes. Others need help with the pains of relational fracture brought through divorce, abuse, or abortion.

So, what tangible arena calls out to you? If you have prevailed through your other seasons of life, and now stand in a time of Impartation, how will you bless your environment as

Jacob did? Think of it: You have the privilege of tapping into your life resources and blessings to help in an arena of need.

My father-in-law was a wonderful example of this to me. Every week, even until the last year of his life, Dad Kirkpatrick dished out soup in the serving line of a local mission. For over 60 years, he touched lives around the world. He was certainly entitled to sit back and relax. But, till the very end, he still had a heart to help those who were hurting. By that kind of faith and service, Dad Kirkpatrick inspired many.

THE INTANGIBLE ARENA

"...And Israel strengthened himself...and he blessed Joseph..."
GENESIS 48:2, 15 NKJV

"...All these are the twelve tribes of Israel, and this is what their father spoke to them. And he blessed them..." **GENESIS 49:28 NKJV**

Jacob laid his hands on his children and blessed them. What a sacred and cherished occasion for the old patriarch, the Impartation of his life purpose to his children and grandchildren. All the wisdom and resources that Jacob had harvested throughout his life would be passed on to the generations that followed.

An intangible arena is the relationship you have with any of those who receive an Impartation of life from you. That arena holds two categories of people.

THE BLOODLINE

First and foremost, the intangible arena includes your own children. Even if they don't realize it yet, they need and await your Impartation.

When parents look back over all the trials and traumas, growth phases, mistakes, achievements, educational paths, and the nights in ERs or police stations, they may not realize that their spiritual deposit was building through every stage.

When parents look back over all the trials and traumas, growth phases, mistakes, achievements, educational paths, and the nights in ERs or police stations, they may not realize that their spiritual deposit was building through every stage.

Yes, I know that some of you are reading this section with a hurting heart. You did your best, but you and your children remain caught in the heartache of a damaged or broken relationship. But, remember there is no relational rupture that God cannot repair. Peter told everyone, *young and old,* to clothe themselves with humility toward one another. He continued, "Therefore humble yourselves under the mighty hand of God, that He may exalt you in due time, casting all your care upon Him, for He cares for you." 1 PETER 5:5 NKJV

I've known many parents who walked through those life passages of pain. When they learned the path of humility, they discovered the last chapter of their parent/child relationship was the best one.

THE HEARTLINE

The intangible arena also includes your spiritual family, those whom the Lord has joined to you for His own purposes, your spiritual sons and daughters. Regardless of age, ethnicity, education, or economic status, they will gather around your table of Impartation, hungry for your word that gives them life!

THE ARROW OF IMPARTATION

Impartation is like an arrow in your hand; you want to hit the target in transmitting your treasure. An arrow has four parts that affect its path to the target.

1. The arrowhead (the tip)
2. The shaft (the long spine)
3. The fletching (the vanes or feathers)
4. The nock (the slot at the rear).

Your Season of Impartation has four corresponding parts that will control its flight and delivery of your payload.

REVELATION

"... he blessed each one according to his own blessing..."
Genesis 49:18 NKJV

Revelation is the arrowhead of the Impartation. When Jacob blessed his sons, he needed a specific message or gift for each one. Jacob needed to impart a delivery that would penetrate the heart of the recipient. For that, he didn't need to pull something out of his "ministry bag"; he needed *revelation!*

Revelation is a supernatural disclosure, an arrow selected by God that will carry a life-changing Impartation to a person. It finds its path through God's radar, identifying a mystery in the heart of the one you are blessing.

Just as the purpose of the arrowhead is to penetrate and cling to the target, revelation is an epiphany from the Lord delivered straight to the heart.

The transmission of your life purpose "arrow" requires two "listens." First, don't assume you know what others need. You must *listen* to the target of your Impartation. And, that begins with asking, *"How can I help you?"* and then hearing what he or she actually says. You don't give what you know; you give what is needed!

> **You don't give what you know; you give what is needed!**

Second, listen to God. He has already been to that person's future, and He knows what he or she needs. God wants to give you a timely and accurate word of the blessing that He has deposited in you.

DISCERNMENT

"…Then Israel (Jacob) stretched out his right hand and laid it on Ephraim's head, who was the younger, and his left hand on Manasseh's head, guiding his hands knowingly, for Manasseh was the firstborn… And Joseph said to his father, 'Not so, my father, for this one is the firstborn; put your right hand on his head.' But his father (Jacob) refused and said, 'I know my son, I know…'"

Genesis 48:14-19 NKJV

As stated previously, the cultural custom directed the Blessing of Birthright to the firstborn. But, it didn't always happen that way. Jacob, for example, received the firstborn blessing because of God's sovereignty, which presided even through Rebekah's manipulation. Now, Jacob was about to impart the Blessing of Birthright, but not to his firstborn son, Reuben. Instead, he blessed Joseph's two sons, Manasseh and Ephraim. Furthermore, Jacob didn't just carry the Blessing of Birthright to Manasseh and Ephraim, he conveyed the Blessing of Promise to Ephraim, Joseph's younger son. Ephraim would be greater, and his descendants would become a multitude of nations.

Discernment interprets God's absolute and precise will, not human emotions. Discernment is not just knowing what to say, but how to say it.

When Joseph saw that Jacob had switched hands on his two sons, he tried to correct his father. But, what Jacob did was deliberate. Jacob had discerned the will of God for the order of blessing. He was operating within God's guidance system.

As with the arrow's shaft, discernment delivers the Word of God with graceful mastery. For example, the old patriarch, Israel (Jacob) would not allow the cultural custom or Joseph's preferences to pull him off course. Discernment interprets God's absolute and precise will, not human emotions. Discernment is not just knowing what to say, but how to say it.

ENCOURAGEMENT

"... By the God of your father who will help you. And by the Almighty who will bless you..." **GENESIS 49:25 NKJV**

Encouragement gives support, confidence, and hope to those who receive the blessing. It stabilizes the heart with courage. Real encouragement does not flow from pop psychology or Hallmark® cards; it is God's confidence delivered in the power of the spoken word.

The purpose of the arrow's fletching is to provide stability and accuracy while in flight. It does this by causing the arrow to spin like a bullet, increasing its penetration of the target. Encouragement is a "fletching" of God's strength that helps your bloodline or heartline to receive the arrow with greater effect.

When God spoke to Moses about his successor, Joshua, He said, "... Encourage him, for he will lead Israel as they take possession of it..." (Deuteronomy 1:38 NLT) The word "encourage" means to fasten upon, seize, cleave to, be obstinate with courage. The enemy wants to stop the transmission of your life purpose to others by *dis*couraging them—breaking their firm attachment to courage. But, your words to, with, and for others can be potent and significant. You can increase that significance through your positive words of encouragement.

Encouragement is more powerful than correction.

Remember, encouragement is more powerful than correction.

MENTORING

"... So he blessed them that day, saying, "By you Israel will bless, saying, 'May God ***make*** *you as Ephraim and as Manasseh' ..."* GENESIS 48:20 NKJV

As Jacob blessed Ephraim and Manasseh, he not only imparted life *to* them, he saw that God wanted to "make" something *in* them. And that would call for mentoring.

The arrow's nock is the slotted connection between the arrow and the bowstring. It maximizes the range and penetration of the arrow. As with the nock, mentoring increases the range and entry of life into your spiritual lineage.

Mentoring is advising, training, and counseling in ways that will enable the mentee to achieve his or her potential. To mentor is to help reproduce God's will and purpose in others. The Season of Impartation is a time when God establishes you in relationships with your spiritual sons and daughters so you can reproduce and develop His magnificence in others.

In the Season of Impartation, we teach, and we mentor. And, there is a difference between the two. Teaching is imparting truth *to* others; mentoring is cultivating truth *in* others. You teach what you know, but you mentor who you are. The Season of Impartation is an extraordinary time; it increases the range, accuracy, and depth of His truth into others.

> Teaching is imparting truth *to* others; mentoring is cultivating truth *in* others. You teach what you know, but you mentor who you are.

I will be forever grateful for my dear friend, Victor Anfuso. As my God-appointed "business mentor," we worked together in the development and operation of CCLI for 24 years. Victor was a successful lawyer from New York who had met several U.S. Presidents (JFK even gave Victor his PT-109 tie clip). He had decades of business knowledge when I had a few years of creative intuition!

But, we were polar opposites in our strengths. After a few months of friction, Victor and I came to a place of wondering if we could even work together. We agreed to pray about it over the weekend and then meet to discuss whatever God might have said to us. When we met, Victor told me what God said to him: "I'm supposed to serve you." Then I shared what God spoke to me: "I'm supposed to put my life in your hands." That day, God knit our hearts together, and I became a grateful "son" and recipient of Victor's wisdom.

The beauty of Impartation enables us to value mentoring relationships more than our independence. It helps us understand mentoring is not about imposing our personal life patterns on others; it is about cultivating God's life and principles in them.

Your life was never any of those individual races. It has always been a relay. You received the baton of your life purpose from the generation before you, and you will pass it to the generation that follows you.

LET US RUN THE RACE

When you first begin the journey, you think life is a 100-yard sprint. You enthusiastically exude unfettered ideas as you dash around with unabated energy. After a while, you reassess your life and think it is a 400-meter run. You just need to extend your "boundless" enthusiasm and energy a little bit further. Later, you see that your life purpose pursuit is actually a 1-mile race. So, you start to pace your personal prowess life-lap by life-lap.

Then, you re-evaluate your race and determine that it is surely a marathon. Your initial surge of life-exhilaration dissipated a long time ago and, now, with the pangs of numbness and exhaustion belaboring you, you summon up enough energy to steadfastly plod on in your life purpose pursuit.

Finally, you realize your life purpose was never any of those individual races. It was never a 100-yard sprint. It was never a 400-meter run. It was never a 1-mile race. It was never a marathon.

It has always been a relay.[23] You received the baton from the generation before you, and you will pass it to the generation that follows you.

Our hope is to have the honor and joy of stepping into David's prayer, "Now that I am old and gray, do not abandon me, O God. Let me proclaim Your power to this new generation, your mighty miracles to all who come after me." **Psalms 71:18 NLT**

The Season of Impartation is the final leg of your life relay—pass your life purpose baton on to those who follow. Finish strong! The heavenly whisper of "Well done!" awaits you from the One who eternally loves you!

May this Mahalia Jackson song permeate your heart during your Season of impartation:

If I can help somebody, as I travel along
If I can help somebody, with a word or song
If I can help somebody, from doing wrong
No, my living shall not be in vain
No, my living shall not be in vain
No, my living shall not be in vain
If I can help somebody, as I'm singing the song
You know, my living shall not be in vain.[24]

EPILOGUE

FOR ALL ETERNITY

Scripture Reference: The Gospel of John

Think of the following pages as my personal letter to you. I did not include it as a chapter because it is so personal.

Here's the deal; I believe God told me to write this to you. Think about that. I was focused on finishing the book; I was not thinking about you.

But, God tapped me on the shoulder. When I stopped to pay attention, I heard Him tell me to invite you to step into deeper purposes in Him than you may have discovered.

Wow; that must mean He loves and cares for you. It may be a good idea to read this. You wouldn't want to miss what He may be saying to you.

"*...When Jacob had finished this charge to his sons, he drew his feet into the bed, breathed his last, and joined his ancestors in death...*" Genesis 49:33 NLT

Jacob, at last, achieved his life's purpose. All the Life Seasons that he embraced, both eagerly and reluctantly, completed God's work in his life. He finished his course and he fought a good fight.

In the end, Jacob declared to his children — "I have been blessed beyond anything I could have ever imagined or desired!" (my paraphrase of Genesis 49:26) After Jacob finished blessing his children, his final act was to worship the Creator of his life and the Lover of his soul. He surely would have agreed with the prophet Daniel: "...Blessed be the name of God forever and ever, for wisdom and might are His. And He changes the times and the seasons..." **Daniel 2:20-21 NKJV**

Jacob was truly a man for all seasons. I hope I have been the same.

We are all passing into, through, or out of a Life Season.

In faithfulness to our God, we must be people for all seasons. God designs them for everyone. Just as they do in the natural, God's spiritual seasons administrate life. Each one performs its own unique work in human life. As a result, we are all passing into, through, or out of a Life Season.

We often do not realize (or we forget) that crises, losses, fears, insecurities, and successes belong to seasons. They are part of His grand administration of life. Each may feel as if it will last forever, but none do. Every season of life on earth has a start and a finish.

When Jacob completed his life and purpose on earth, his life was not over. He joined his ancestors on the other side of eternity. And there, Jacob began another season, one that has no end. That is the Season of Original Promise, the place where God's children enjoy what David described in Psalm 16:11 NKJV: "In Your presence *is* fullness of joy; At Your right hand *are* pleasures forevermore."

What is your eternal season going to be like?

As much as I hope this book carries value for you in your pursuit of your life's purpose on earth, my deeper hope for the readers of this book is that each of you will discover His purpose for you in the great continuum of life throughout eternity.

I'm hopeful that most have already embraced the "forever and ever" joy of the eternal season. But, there might be some of you who don't know what I'm talking about. Perhaps you don't even know why you bought this book. Maybe someone gave it to you.

But, that's not the end of the story. Jesus Christ triumphed over death and sin, and rose again! Because of that great truth, God's eternal life became once again available to everyone.

I must ask: Do you know that God created you to dwell with Him? That was God's original design for all people. That's how life on earth actually began. There was no hardship, pain, sadness, sorrow, or stress; no worries, sickness, or disease. Just "pleasures forevermore" with God.

So, what happened?

The first man, Adam, and his wife, Eve, really screwed up (it's called "sin"). They committed such a horrible breach of trust — they disobeyed God — that all of humanity was banned from God's "forevermore." And, because of this separation from God's eternal purpose, all of us now suffer the consequences — we "all have sinned" (Romans 3:23) and are alienated from God's original intent for us.

That's when and why all the life mess began.

But, God did not want to let us permanently dwell in the slimy muck of misery. He didn't want us to be "doom-damned." God had a plan to rescue us, and here's the incredibly great news: God. Loves. You! In fact, God loves you so much that He gave

His only Son, Jesus, to come to earth and fix the breach. And, He took *your* sin upon himself, was crucified, and buried. The Son of God died.

But, that's not the end of the story. Jesus Christ triumphed over death and sin, and rose again! Because of that great truth, God's eternal life became once again available to everyone.

Entrance into life's "forever pleasure" is found and accessed through this simple prayer:

Don't let your yesterday be the barrier to your tomorrow.

"Jesus, I believe you are the Son of God. Thank you for giving your life for me. Forgive me for my sin. Come into my heart. I accept you as my Savior. I receive your promise to live with you in the forever pleasure on the other side of eternity."

Welcome to the family!

But wait, there's more; God wants your life to be full of joy now...on earth. He has so much that He wants to share with you about your life's purpose. You can discover your brand-new life now.

Are you ready to get started? Please go to www.thepurplebook.org and download the first lesson free. You can now begin to enjoy the nourishment for your future!

Maybe you already know everything that I have shared here. Perhaps you once had a personal relationship with Jesus Christ. But, you messed up, veered off-course, gave up, and have now classified yourself as an incorrigible, unredeemable soul.

Guess what? God still loves you! It's not over. God's arms are wide open, ready to welcome you once again into His eternal family. Come home! Don't let your yesterday be the barrier to your tomorrow.

Just tell God you are sorry and that you want to give your life to Him again. Then, get ready for His amazing grace to embrace you.

I may never have the privilege of meeting you personally. But, if this book has helped you, I would love to hear from you. Please email me at:

Perpetual@HowardRachinski.com

Don't ever forget that God designed your life and its purpose. And, He did so with great purpose and precision. He also designed the seasons of life. Just like the natural seasons, they serve as vital instruments of His administration of His creation, including you!

Discover the beauty and wisdom of the seasons. Embrace them. Allow them to perform His perfect work in you. Enjoy your life journey. For all eternity.

ACKNOWLEDGMENTS

The great preacher, Ern Baxter, once said, "Writing a book is like giving birth to an elephant." He wasn't kidding.

Now that the elephant has been born, please indulge me while I express my gratefulness to those who have played a significant role in my life journey and in the writing and delivery of this "baby."

To my wife, Donna Gem—I have been blessed beyond all comprehension to have you as my beautiful God-given soulmate. You shared every moment and endured every season with me. Many times, your intercessory prayers carried me through; knowing that you believed in me gave me the courage to persevere. Thank you for being my hand-holder...*Gwa ai lee*!!!

To my children, Dyane, Deryk, and Dryden, what a delight it is for me to be called your Dad. And, there is nothing you can do about that! Ha ha ha... Mom and I learned so much about His unfailing love as we did life together with you. You are the greatest blessings that God has given to us, and I pray that your Life Seasons have been enriched by the treasures we tried to deposit into your hearts. And, to Dyane's twin, whom we lost in miscarriage, we never had the joy of holding you in our arms here on earth, but we look forward to meeting you in heaven.

To our wonderful grandchildren, Judah, Delaney, Carter, Sawyer, Stella, Sydney, and Elyza (and more to come!), thank you for making Eagle Crest and Maui vacations such a wonderful family time. Opa loves you and is praying that you all will flourish through your Life Seasons as you pursue His Calling for your life.

Without a doubt, Donna and I were blessed with an amazing heritage! To my parents, Ernie and Ida Rachinski, thank you for all your years of loving sacrifice that made Myrna, Rod, and I feel so special. Your investment in us is for all eternity! You showed me how to be a man of God and a lover of His Presence. I love you! To my in-laws, James and Patricia Kirkpatrick, thank you for welcoming me into your heart and for showing me the joy of faithful service. We really miss you, I'm hoping God will allow you to read this up there.

To all the Rachinski "tribe"—aunts, uncles, nieces, nephews, in-laws and out-laws—thank you for being "family"! I am so glad that we are "blood!"

When you read this book, you will know that my prime Season of Productivity was during my CCLI years. I had the highest privilege of walking together with some dear and wonderful men and women. Thank you, Victor and Kathy Anfuso, for being such a blessing to me! I will always be grateful for Victor's mentoring in my life; our 24 years of working together are loaded with cherished memories. Thank you to every Executive Team member throughout the years—Malcolm Hawker (my successor), Andy Bodkin, Geoff Booker, Gary Christensen, Dave Dickenson, Bruce Groshong, Pete Ittner, Shari Iverson, Terry Iverson, Rod Rachinski, Piers Ramsay,

George Ross, and Michael Thelander—for faithfully pursuing the vision with me. Thank you to every Board member—Victor Anfuso, Doug Crane, Frank Damazio, Dick Iverson, Art Johansen, Jack Louman, Keith Meyers, Phil Perkins, Craig Smith and Mark Reed—for your amazing guidance and counsel.

Thank you to everyone in the CCLI family. I will never forget all the fun we had, the picnics, retreats, birthday parties, Christmas banquets, snowball fights, weekly devotions, prayer breakthroughs, laughter, and tears. It was an honor to serve as your CEO, and I pray that our moments together brought enrichment to your respective Life Seasons.

I also thank those spiritual fathers and wise counselors who have invested their lives into my heart: Reg Layzell, Dick Iverson, Frank Damazio, Marc Estes, Lew & Marion Peterson, Glen Roachelle, David Crabtree, Andraé Crouch, and Sandra Crouch. Thank you for your treasured life engravement! May I faithfully impart to others what you have deposited into me.

Thank you to all my close and dear friends who have traveled with me in my life purpose. There are too many to name individually. But, you know who you are... Thank you!

This book would have never become a reality without one very special and gifted friend, Ed Chinn. Thank you so much for your skillful navigation through the "elephant delivery." Your steadfast patience and encouragement sustained me when I felt writer's exasperation. I am so grateful for your imprint on this book!

And, I appreciate Faye Beaulieu for her copyediting, Bill Kersey for his design work, and the reviewers—Duke Bendix, Gary Christensen, Susan Crainshaw, Craig Dahlberg, Mark Duggin, Jerry and MarySue Hermes, Sue Long, Glenda Malmin, Stan Moser, Joseph Partain, Kara Paulus, Glen Roachelle, Dale Smith, and Tom Sutter for your skillful review of this book. I am honored that you would take the time to assess my words so that they can better shift from the paper to the heart.

Finally (but first and foremost), thank you, God, for never giving up on me! I can't live without your Presence, and I promise to passionately pursue YOU through all my Life Seasons.

ENDNOTES

1. Retief, Frank. *Tragedy To Triumph: A Christian Response To Trials And Suffering.* Milton Keynes: Nelson Word, 1994.
2. *Ibid.*
3. *John Wesley's Notes on the Bible,* Benediction Classics, 2010.
4. http://wonderopolis.org/wonder/why-are-all-snowflakes-different
5. R. Jamieson, *Jamieson, Fausset, and Brown's Commentary On the Whole Bible* (Zondervan, 1999)
6. https://www.quora.com/How-is-salt-made.
7. Chris Tiegreen, *The One Year At His Feet Devotional* (Tyndale Momentum, 2006)
8. Seneca, *On the Shortness of Life: Life Is Long if You Know How to Use It* (New York: Penguin Books, 2005)
9. https://www.merriam-webster.com/dictionary/famine.
10. https://www.theguardian.com/science/blog/2018/mar/14/why-humans-are-optimised-for-endurance-running-not-speed.
11. Strong, J. (1890). *Strong's Exhaustive Concordance of the Bible.* New York, NY: Abingdon Press.
12. http://www.eaec.org/faithhallfame/fanny_crosby.htm
13. http://www.eaec.org/faithhallfame/fanny_crosby.htm
14. John Ruskin, *Sesame and Lilies; The Ethics of the Dust; The Crown of Wild Olive: With Letters on Public Affairs,* 1859-1866 (John Wiley & Sons, 1891)
15. https://www.webmd.com/balance/stress-management/effects-of-stress-on-your-body

[16] Ellen Goodman, "Letting Go, and Looking Ahead," January 1, 2010, The Boston Globe

[17] https://www.merriam-webster.com/dictionary/revive

[18] *NKJV*

[19] Strong, J. (1890). *Strong's Exhaustive Concordance of the Bible.* New York, NY: Abingdon Press.

[20] Ibid.

[21] *NKJV*

[22] https://www.merriam-webster.com/dictionary/famine

[23] A similar version of this statement was shared to me by my friend, Dan Burr

[24] Written by Alma Androzzo, Public Domain